How to make

Pillows

By the Editors of Sunset Books and Sunset Magazine

Lane Publishing Co. • Menlo Park, California

Special thanks to...

the designers whose names appear in the photo captions, and to the following persons and places for their generous assistance and wonderful ideas: Leslie Batchelor, Marinda Brown, Toni Carner, BFJ's Collectanea, The Cotton Works, Karen Cummings, Designcrafts of California, Pierre Deux, Judy Frost, Susan Gregory, House of Today, Sudha Irwin, Kneedler-Fauchere, Margaret Laycock, Karen Loy, Marimekko, Inc., Hank Morgan, Norah's Sewing, The Right Touch, Jane Sims, Tallman's House of Foam, Nancy Welch, and Laurel Wilson.

Book Editor:
Christine Barnes

Staff Editors:
Suzy Warton
Kathy Arthurs

Editorial Consultant:
Sharon Multhauf

Design:
Sandra Popovich

Photography:
Steve W. Marley

Illustrations:
Sally Shimizu
Sandra Popovich

Cover: Plump sunburst pillow and a trio of bordered mock-box pillows decorate a cozy window seat cushion. All are done in coordinated fabrics and trims for an impressive—and varied—pillow collection. Design: Benita McConnell. Photographed by Steve W. Marley.

Editor, Sunset Books:
David E. Clark

Contents

4–31 Pillow Techniques

Before you begin   4
How to make pillows   16
How to make cushions   28
How to make bolsters   30

32–49 Pillow Decorating Ideas

50–79 Pillow Projects

Gift-wrapped pillows   50
Herbal heirloom pillows   51
Woven ribbon pillow   54
Let a child design your pillow   56
Ribbon-linked pillow train   57
Crewel landscape pillows   59
Mola pillow   60
Art nouveau pillow   62
Summer & winter pillows   64
Smocked pillow   66
Shiki-buton   68
Tube-quilted mat   70
Printed & painted pillows   72
Lemon & orange chair pillow   73
Early American stencil pillow   75
A quartet of patchwork baskets   76
Breakfast-in-bed bolsters   78

80 Index

Pillow Techniques

Arranged on a sofa, tossed on the floor, piled high on a bed or bench, strewn on a patio—pillows belong wherever you put them.

A quick look through this book will show you that pillow possibilities, both decorative and functional, are unlimited.

Populate an entire room with a collection of bright, playful pillows... or just enjoy stitching a special piece of pillow art for yourself or for someone else.

Whatever your pillow plans, this chapter offers you the means to carry them out. Beginning on page 16 are step-by-step instructions for making roomfuls of pillows, cushions, and bolsters, with variations such as gathered pillow corners, shirred cushion boxing, and pleated bolster ends to give your pillows that custom-made look.

The techniques for pillow-making are all assembled here; the imagination and creativity are up to you. Look over the information, select a pillow style, gather your materials, and stitch away. Wherever you decide your pillows belong, they're sure to fit right in.

Before you begin

In this section you'll find important tips on tools you'll need and on fabric suitability and selection, plus invaluable instructions for calculating and cutting fabric. You'll also learn about pillow forms and fillers, and about such techniques as making welt and installing zippers—techniques you'll use again and again in pillow-making.

Before you begin, browse through these next pages to review—or discover—some pillow basics. With a little preparation, the time spent from inspiration to finished pillow will be shorter, and a lot more fun.

Sewing tools & supplies

One of the great pleasures of pillow-making is the simplicity of the sewing. With just a few basic tools and a little sewing skill, you can stitch up simple pillows in no time at all. Even the more complex pillows, cushions, and bolsters are done with the same equipment and stitching skills. If you've done any sewing at all, you're sure to be able to follow our instructions successfully.

Before you cut or sew, gather together the equipment you'll need. Following is a list of the basic sewing tools and supplies that will enable you to turn your pillow fantasies into realities to use, admire, and enjoy.

Measuring tools

The beginnings of a well-made square or rectangular pillow are straight, pillow pieces with perfect right-angle corners. A *drafting triangle* or *carpenter's square* is very helpful for squaring off the ends of fabric. You can buy a triangle at an art supply store and a square at a hardware store.

A *yardstick* is useful for making long cutting lines; a 12-inch *ruler* is more convenient for making shorter measurements and lines. Make sure each is smooth (so it won't snag fabric) and straight.

To mark fabric, use *chalk* or a *wax pencil*, available in the notions sections of fabric, variety, and department stores. Avoid pencils that leave permanent marks after pressing. Experiment on a sample piece of fabric—if the mark remains after pressing and it won't sponge off, use a different pencil.

Cutting tools

Easier on the hands than regular scissors, *bent-handle shears* allow fabric to lie flat while you cut. Choose a pair that is 8 or 9 inches long; they're easy to handle and the blades cut quickly. Be strict about using your shears only on fabric (paper will dull the blades quickly).

About 4 inches long, *embroidery scissors* are handy for making cuts in welt seam allowances when turning corners and for clipping threads while sewing. *Thread clips* are even more convenient to use for snipping threads.

Ironing tools

A *steam iron* is necessary for pressing pillow edges and slightly puckered welt.

For best pressing results, make sure that your *ironing board* is adequately padded. A *press cloth* of unbleached muslin laid over the pillow fabric protects it from scorch and iron shine.

Sewing tools

Your *sewing machine* is probably your most important piece of sewing equipment. Take care of your machine, oiling and cleaning it as directed by your manual, and your machine will reward you with consistently good stitching. If you're getting less-than-perfect results, check threading, tension, and stitch length; minor adjustments according to manual

instructions will correct most problems.

A *zipper foot* is a must for stitching welt to a pillow and for installing a zipper.

A strip of *masking tape*, placed parallel to the line of stitching, makes a handy seam guide. To the right of the needle, measure the distance of your seam allowance (½ inch for most seams, ¾ inch for zipper seams, and ¼ inch for several exceptions). Place a 6-inch strip of tape with its left-hand edge at this point. As you sew, line up the seam allowances with the edge of the tape. This guide is especially helpful when you're topstitching a flange.

Use *machine needles* that are compatible with the weight and type of your fabric; needle packages and your manual will guide your selection. For handstitching closures, you'll need a package of *hand-sewing needles* in assorted sizes. An *upholstery needle* can be helpful for tufting.

Fine, sharp *dressmaker pins*, about 1¼ inches long and made of stainless steel, are best but sometimes hard to find. Stronger than dressmaker pins are *T-pins*, helpful for holding plush or open-weave fabrics, which tend to swallow pins with standard heads. Use *safety pins* to pull cord through casings.

Fibers, fabric & care

Pillow-making allows you tremendous freedom with fabrics. Because pillows are easy and relatively inexpensive to make, you can indulge your imagination and creativity in fabric texture, pattern, and color. Here's your chance to splurge on a luxurious fabric, to mix complementary patterns, or to introduce a striking color into a neutral room.

Fabric considerations

To help you choose from among the inspiring—and sometimes

overwhelming—assortment of fabrics, consider the following fabric questions.

• *Is the fabric suited to the pillow's use?* A firmly woven fabric that retains its shape is a must for pillows that will receive normal to heavy use. Loose weaves have a lovely texture but are best for decorative pillows rather than hard-working ones. Also consider durability—some fibers and fabrics (especially synthetics and blends) wear longer than others.

• *Is the fabric suited to the decorative technique?* If you plan to embellish your pillow, pick a fabric appropriate to the technique. Embroidery, for example, requires a firmly woven fabric; reverse appliqué is most successful with an all-cotton fabric that holds a crease. Ask a salesperson for advice on suitable fabrics if the technique is new to you.

• *Is the fabric fade-resistant?* Outdoor cushions or pillows destined for a sunny spot will look tired long before you're tired of them if you choose a fabric that fades. The dye process used for a fabric determines its resistance to the fading effects of sun. Vat-dyeing produces the best results; surface-dyed or printed fabrics have the least resistance to fading. Generally, dark colors fade faster and more than light ones.

• *Is the fabric easily cleaned?* With fabrics made of such fibers as silk, wool, and acetate, you usually have no choice but to dry-clean. Most of the fabrics you're likely to use for pillows are washable, but remember that washing tends to remove finishes and will shrink some fabrics. Dry-cleaning these fabrics, though less convenient and more costly, will preserve the finish.

Fibers into fabric

Before you consider fabric color or pattern, think first about fiber— the raw material from which the fabric is made. Each fiber has certain distinct characteristics, and often several fibers are blended to produce a fabric with the best qualities of each fiber.

Natural fibers. Those who favor natural fibers insist that man can't make them the way nature has. For the most part, natural fibers feel good, both at first touch and after years of use. Increasingly available and popular again, the natural fibers—cotton, linen, silk, and wool—make up the preferred fabrics for pillows because they wear well and retain their shape better than most synthetics. They are also easy to work with and, with the exception of wool, are comfortable next to your skin.

The main drawbacks to natural fibers are their tendency to shrink, wrinkle, and fade. Only you can evaluate these disadvantages against the great advantages of sewing and living with fabrics made from natural fibers.

Synthetic fibers. Though no longer considered "wonder fibers," as they were several decades ago, synthetics are durable and easy to care for. The qualities you sacrifice with synthetics are comfort and a certain ease of handling that makes the natural fibers such a pleasure to work with. Stitching a boxing strip to a pillow top or bottom, for example, is more difficult with a synthetic that doesn't give than with a natural fiber that will ease or stretch slightly to fit.

Acetate, acrylic, nylon, polyester, and rayon are the most commonly used synthetics. You're not likely to choose a fabric made from just one of these fibers, but many fabrics that appear to be "natural" are in reality blends of natural and synthetic fibers. Perhaps the most popular of these is polyester and cotton.

Generalizations about synthetic fibers are difficult because their significant characteristics vary so much. Most synthetics are durable and washable; most also retain their shape with use and wrinkle less than natural fibers. On the negative side, synthetics are usually uncomfortable. Acetate and rayon are exceptions—both tend to wrinkle and must be dry-cleaned, but they are comfortable next to the skin.

Fabric shopping

Chances are you already have a fabric pattern or color in mind for your pillow, cushion, or bolster. You may have seen a particular fabric you like, or you may plan to coordinate your pillows with what you already have.

You'll probably find the best fabric selection in large fabric stores, many of which carry decorator fabrics. Other sources are interior designers, department store fabric departments, and drapery and upholstery shops.

If possible, take along paint chips and fabric swatches to compare colors, textures, and patterns. Better still, buy a small piece of a fabric you're considering (most stores will sell you ⅛ yard) and try it out at home. It's worth the cost and trouble, for a change in background color and lighting can significantly alter the appearance of fabric. You can also test how the fabric sews and whether or not it wrinkles.

Check fabric grain. No matter how large or small the pillow, you'll get the best results—from cutting to final stitching—if your fabric has a straight grain (crosswise threads running precisely perpendicular to lengthwise threads). Avoid printed fabric that is severely off-grain—the finished pillow, cushion, or bolster will look crooked, and the seams may pucker.

To check patterned fabric in the store, fold the fabric back a few inches across the grain, with wrong sides together and selvages aligned. If the print runs evenly along the fold, it is fairly well aligned with the fabric grain.

Choosing thread. Polyester thread and cotton-wrapped polyester thread, both available in a wide range of colors, are the most commonly used. Choose polyester thread for most synthetics. For fabrics of natural fibers and blends, cotton-wrapped polyester thread is excellent; it combines the best qualities of polyester and mercerized cotton and is very strong.

Choose thread that is a slightly darker shade than your fabric; for prints, use thread that matches the predominant color.

To preshrink or not?

As a rule, you should preshrink your fabric before cutting if you expect ever to wash the finished pillow cover. Keep in mind, though, that preshrinking and washing will destroy some of the finish with which the fabric is treated; besides losing its fresh, crisp appearance, the fabric will lose some of the properties the finish provides. Polished cotton, for example, will lose some of its sheen and may soil more easily. If preserving the fabric's finish is important to you, it may be worth the effort and expense to have a dry-cleaner run the fabric through a steamer (to shrink the fabric with minimal change in its finish) and then dry-clean your finished pillow when necessary.

Pressing tips

There's no getting around it—to get a professional-looking pillow, you must pay attention to details and press as you sew. Always test a small piece of the fabric beforehand to determine how much heat, moisture, and pressure from the iron will produce smooth results without damaging the fabric.

Safe ironing temperatures vary according to fiber content. If your fabric is a blend, let its most delicate fiber dictate the heat level to use. To be safe, begin on low and increase the temperature until you get the results you want.

A press cloth prevents scorch and iron shine. Covering the ironing board with extra padding, such as flannel or another soft fabric, will provide additional protection for heat-sensitive fabrics. Finally, to be safe, press the wrong side of the fabric. (*Never* press the right side if the fabric is embossed, glazed, or highly textured, or if it has been painted or embroidered.)

Fabric calculations & cutting

Pillow-making begins here, with calculations for the necessary fabric, and with careful measuring, marking, and cutting of the pillow pieces. These preliminary steps are critical, for fabric cut with even slightly crooked lines will produce a finished pillow that looks disturbingly lopsided and unprofessional.

How much fabric will you need?

Decide first on the style and size of your pillow, cushion, or bolster. The illustrations and descriptions in this chapter will help you choose from among the many pillow possibilities. Size will be up to you, but keep in mind that a filled pillow appears significantly larger than its flat pieces. As a general guide, a good finished size for a square throw pillow is 14 by 14 inches; a floor pillow or cushion looks good about 24 by 24 inches. A bolster generally needs to fit a specific bed, window seat, or piece of furniture, though a typical form length is 36 inches, with a diameter of 9 inches for a round bolster, or a height of 12 inches for a wedge bolster.

In determining the size of your pillow, cushion, or bolster, it pays to consider fabric width. For example, you can cut two 10-inch pillows from a length of 45-inch-wide fabric. For two 14-inch pillows, you would have to buy considerably more fabric because the two could not be cut side by side across the width.

Here's how to figure the amount of fabric to buy: For a knife-edge pillow, you will need enough fabric for top and bottom pieces. A boxed cushion requires enough fabric for the top and bottom, plus a boxing strip whose length equals the cushion's perimeter or circumference plus 6 inches. For a bolster you'll need enough fabric to encircle the round, rectangular, or wedge form, plus fabric for the end pieces. Cut top and bottom pieces the *exact size* of the form, adding ¼ inch to zipper edges if you plan to install a zipper.

If you want to outline your pillow, cushion, or bolster edges with welt, see pages 9–10 to determine how much fabric you'll need for the bias casing. Refer to the specific pillow technique instructions to calculate yardage for such extras as ruffles, flanges, or sham closures.

With fabric that has a one-way design or a large repeat motif, be sure to allow enough extra fabric to cut the pieces with the pattern in the desired direction or with the motifs centered.

After allowing fabric for all of the pieces and any trim, add several inches for good measure. If you plan to preshrink your fabric before cutting, allow a few more inches. Round the number of inches up to the nearest ⅛ yard to establish the amount of fabric to buy.

Measuring, marking & cutting

Follow the appropriate instructions below to cut square, rectangular, or round pillow pieces.

Square or rectangular pieces. Your first step is to square off one cut end of fabric. With right sides together, press fabric. Using a straightedge, mark (with soft pencil or chalk—never pen) a straight line parallel and close to selvages or one lengthwise edge.

If fabric is patterned, the pattern may be slightly off-grain. On a small pillow, it probably won't matter, but on a long cushion or bolster, misalignment may be jarring. To correct it, open fabric right side up and mark a line following crosswise lines of pattern rather than lengthwise grain; trim fabric along this line. Fold fabric in half lengthwise, with crosswise edges aligned.

Align one arm or side of a carpenter's square or a drafting triangle along lengthwise line

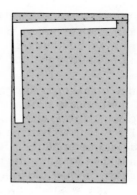

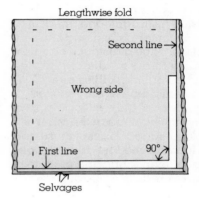

you marked or the crosswise line you trimmed, at a point where you'll be able to draw a line slightly longer than pillow's side. Draw a line perpendicular to your first line or cut; use a straightedge to extend this line as far as necessary.

Use each line as a point from which to measure and mark lines for the other two sides. (Be sure to allow extra fabric at zipper edges; see "Zippers," pages 12–13, for specific allowances on different zipper styles.) Connect marks to complete lines of pillow's perimeter. With square or triangle, check to see that each corner is a true right angle.

If your fabric is a solid or has a small pattern, you can cut out both pieces at the same time. But if the fabric has a large pattern or dominant motif that must be centered, open out fabric and cut top and bottom pieces separately so you can match patterns or center motifs.

Round pieces. There are two ways of cutting round pillow or cushion pieces—one method for a plain circular top or bottom piece, and one for two half-circle bottom pieces to be joined with a lapped zipper.

If you're not using a zipper, the simplest method is to start with a square piece of fabric with sides at least 1 inch longer than the pillow *form's* diameter. Right sides together, fold square in half and press a sharp crease; fold in half again, in opposite direction, and press another sharp crease. (If fabric won't crease firmly, place a row of pins parallel to the fold.) Using a straightedge, measure from center point along one folded edge a distance equal to pillow form's radius (or half the diameter); mark this point. Continue marking evenly spaced points from the center point in an arc until you reach the other folded edge. Connect these points with a curved line and cut along line. Open fabric and press to remove creases.

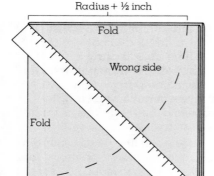

Radius + ½ inch

Fold

Wrong side

Fold

Fold

If you're using a zipper in a round bottom piece, you must cut two half-circles, each with a ¾-inch zipper seam allowance on the straightedge. Start with a square piece of fabric with sides at least 2½ inches longer than pillow *form's* diameter. Fold this square in half and press a sharp crease. Place a row of pins parallel to and about 1½ inches away from fold; cut fabric along fold. Using a straightedge, measure and mark a line ¾ inch from cut

edges; mark midpoint of this line. With this point as center, measure along line a distance equal to pillow form's radius (or half the diameter); mark this point. Continue marking evenly spaced points from center point in an arc until you reach other part of line. Connect these points with a curved line. Within ¾-inch zipper seam allowances, continue the circular line as a straight line. Cut both pieces along line.

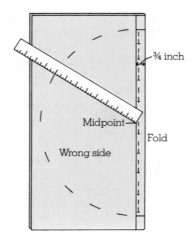

¾ inch

Midpoint

Fold

Wrong side

Boxing strips. For a boxed cushion, measure and mark boxing strip(s) the appropriate length and depth (see "Boxed cushion with welt," page 28, to determine boxing strip dimensions). If possible, cut boxing strips on lengthwise grain of fabric.

Forms & fillers

Though not the least bit glamorous, the forms and fillers that give pillows, cushions, and bolsters their shape have a lot to do with the way the finished pillow will look. Before you begin making the pillow cover, give some thought to the appearance and feel you want to achieve; also consider the purpose the pillow will serve.

You have two options when it comes to forms—you can purchase a ready-made form or make your own. Many pillowmakers find the ready-made forms satisfactory—and using

them certainly is simpler than making your own. Round polyurethane foam forms are typically available in diameters ranging from 12 to 18 inches; square forms come in 12 to 30-inch sizes. Cylindrical and wedge foam bolster forms are usually 36 inches long, with varying diameters and heights.

One caution about readymade forms: they are often larger (by 1 or 2 inches) than the size given for the form. If you want a specific size form (for one of the projects, for example), take a tape measure and check the actual size before you buy.

If you want to make a pillow, cushion, or bolster that has a different size, shape, or feel than a ready-made form, you will have to make your own form.

To determine what size pillow form to buy or make, you must first decide on the finished size you want your pillow, cushion, or bolster to measure. Then, to ensure a smooth, wrinkle-free pillow, you'll need a pillow form 1 inch *larger* than the desired finished size of the pillow. For example, if you want a knife-edge pillow with a finished size of 14 by 14 inches, the form you buy or make must be 15 by 15 inches.

Generally, the pillow form should be the same style as the cover—a knife-edge form for a knife-edge pillow, a boxed or mock-box form for a boxed cushion. Those styles that have a boxing depth without a separate boxing strip can take either a boxed or mock-box form.

If you're using or making a form with a surface of polyurethane foam, either plain or wrapped with *unbonded* polyester batting, you'll find that an extra cloth cover of muslin or similar fabric will make it easier to insert and remove the form. Follow the basic pillow or cushion instructions for the appropriate style to make a muslin case.

Following is information on materials available for pillow forms and fillers, plus instructions for making your own forms.

Polyester filling, probably the most popular of all filler materials, comes packaged loose (usually in 1-pound bags), shaped or stuffed into ready-made forms, or pressed into sheets called batting. Clean, easy to use, and relatively inexpensive, it can be found in most fabric stores and needlework supply shops.

Sewing a muslin or similar-fabric cover and stuffing it with polyester filling is a simple and quick way to get the pillow form you need. Follow the appropriate pillow instructions to stitch a muslin case in the same or a similar style.

A couple of tips: For a smooth pillow, take a fist-size wad of filling from the bag, then gently pull it apart to fluff and separate the fibers. When stuffing the muslin cover, use a large, blunt crochet hook or knitting needle to coax the filling into the corners. Avoid overfilling the form.

For an even smoother surface, instead of using muslin, sew a case from polyester batting and stuff it with loose filling. Look for "bonded" batting—the surface has been treated with a resin to lock the fibers together. If one side of the batting feels firmer than the other, make sure the firmer surface ends up on the outside. Cut the pieces the *exact size* of the desired finished form; with a zigzag stitch, sew ¼ inch from edges. Finish as you would a knife-edge pillow (see pages 16–18).

Polyurethane foam is useful alone or in combination with polyester filling and batting. You can buy foam in sheets, chunks, precut forms, and shreds. (We don't recommend using shreds because they are messy and produce lumpy forms.) Many fabric stores and needlework supply shops carry foam; major department store mail-order catalogs also offer foam. Your best source, though, is a shop specializing in foam; check the Yellow Pages under "Rubber—Foam and Sponge."

The firmness of the foam depends on its density (usually between 1 and 3.5 pounds per cubic foot); generally, the greater the density, the firmer and less resilient the foam will be, but the longer it will last before deteriorating. Some foam shops carry a high-resiliency foam that is both soft and durable. It costs more than other foams, but it's ideal for pillows.

If you buy a chunk of foam for a cushion or bolster, have a foam shop cut it for you, or you can cut it yourself with a serrated knife or, better yet, an electric knife. A spray of silicone lubricant on the blade will help you get a smooth cut.

To soften the contours of a foam form for a pillow, boxed cushion, or bolster, yet maintain the basic shape, you can wrap the foam with one or more layers of polyester batting, either bonded or unbonded. For a more luxurious effect, try to find quilted polyester, several layers of billowy batting loosely quilted to a nonwoven polyester cover. Check the Yellow Pages for "Upholsterers' Supplies."

The procedure is much like gift-wrapping a package: Cut a large enough sheet of batting to cover the foam piece and the ends, spray the foam with adhesive to prevent shifting, and fit the batting around the foam form. Tuck and trim the ends and long edges as needed to eliminate bunching, then whipstitch (see page 14) the edges together.

Kapok, a vegetable fiber, is the filling many decorators and upholsterers like because it fills softly and completely. Though full and fluffy when new, however, a kapok pillow will gradually flatten as the fibers deteriorate. Kapok's fine texture makes it tricky to work with; if this is the pillow filler you want, have an upholsterer make and fill a form for you.

Down, the soft, quill-less feathers from the breast of a goose or duck, is probably the ultimate in pillow luxury. Though very expensive in its pure form, down is often mixed with other fine feathers to produce a more affordable, but still desirable, filler. Because down, like kapok, is difficult to handle, it's best to have an upholsterer make a form for you.

Welt

Welt, sometimes called "welting" or "piping," is the traditional edge trim for pillows, cushions, and bolsters. In addition to being decorative, welt reinforces pillow seams and helps keep edges straight.

You can make your own welt, using the instructions that follow, or, if you prefer, use ready-made welt that contrasts with or complements your pillow's fabric. Ready-made welt comes both packaged and by the yard from continuous rolls in upholstery supply stores and some fabric stores.

How much welt will you need?

A knife-edge pillow requires a length of cord or ready-made welt equal to the pillow's finished perimeter or circumference plus 3 inches for joining welt ends. For a boxed cushion, double the perimeter or circumference and add 6 inches. Treat bolster ends like top and bottom cushion pieces—you'll need welt equal to double the end perimeter or circumference plus 6 inches.

Making your own welt

If you plan to make your own welt, buy plain cord—sometimes called "cable cord"—from a fabric store. You will find cotton or polyester cord in various diameters. For most pillows, cushions, and bolsters, use ¼-inch-thick cord; large floor pillows or cushions look best with thicker welt. Many fabric stores carry thick cord for edging bedspreads, tablecloths, and large pillows.

Using a bias-cut casing of fabric to cover the cord ensures that the welt will fit smoothly around the curves and corners of your pillows or cushions. The bias casing must be wide enough to wrap around the cord, with enough extra for twice the width of the seam allowance. The following instructions, which are based on ¼-inch-thick cord and ½-inch seam allowances, call for a bias casing that's 1⅝ inches wide. Experiment to determine the necessary casing width if you're using a different size cord.

If you're making several pillows or cushions and need a great deal of welt, it's a good idea to make the casing as one continuous bias strip. To do just one pillow, it's simpler to cut and seam separate bias strips for welt. You can cut casing strips on the straight grain if you're short of fabric or if welt will look better cut from the straight grain. Such welt may pucker, though, especially around corners.

Cutting continuous bias casing

In terms of both fabric and effort, this method for making a continuous bias casing is very efficient. The chart at right, above, shows the approximate number of yards you will get from a given amount of fabric.

1. Make bias cylinder. Trim off selvages and fold fabric in half across shorter dimension, right sides together. Stitch a ½-inch seam around the three open sides of the rectangle.

Trim all four corners as shown, cutting through stitching.

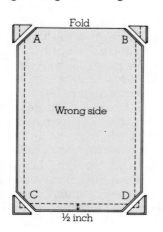

From this much fabric...	...you'll get about this many running yards of 1⅝-inch-wide continuous bias casing		
	36" fabric	48" fabric	54" fabric
¼ yard	4½ yards	5½ yards	7 yards
½ yard	10 yards	13 yards	14 yards
¾ yard	16 yards	20 yards	22 yards
1 yard	22 yards	26 yards	29½ yards

Picking up two diagonally opposite corners (B and C), fold fabric rectangle so it forms two triangles. Carefully insert shears into end of fold and cut through one layer of fabric, all the way across.

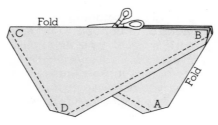

Pick up bottom corners (A and D) and slowly pull them, shaking out fabric; bottom corners are now top corners of a rectangle, with a fold along the top. Smooth fabric so A–D fold is straight.

Cut top fold open so fabric is now a bias cylinder with a fold at each end. Press seam allowances

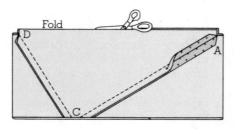

open and trim upper and lower edges of cylinder to make them straight.

2. Measure and mark strips. With chalk or pencil, draw a line across the cylinder perpendicular to and 6 inches from the left-hand

fold. Measure and mark 1⅝-inch-wide strips from the 6-inch line to the opposite end. If you end with a fraction of a strip on the bottom, cut it all the way off cylinder and discard.

3. Cut strips. Cut along marks from right-hand fold to 6-inch line, cutting through both thicknesses of cylinder. After cutting all strips, refold cylinder so that uncut portion is centered on top.

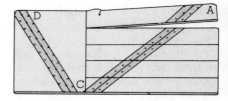

Using a straightedge, mark a diagonal line from end of topmost cut to a point on upper edge of cylinder even with opposite ends of cuts. Next, mark a diagonal line from end of second cut to opposite end of first cut. Continue marking until all cuts are connected with diagonal lines.

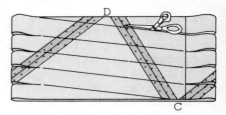

Cutting through one layer of fabric, cut along each diagonal strip. As you do, casing will fall into one continuous bias strip.

Cutting separate bias strips

If you need only a small amount of welt for one or two pillows, here's how to cut and piece separate bias strips.

1. Establish bias line. Fold a corner of fabric so that selvage aligns with crosswise cut; press this bias fold and cut fabric along fold.

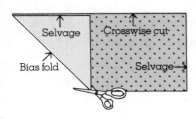

2. Measure, mark, and cut strips. Using diagonal cut as a guideline, measure and mark 1⅝-inch-wide strips parallel to the cut. Stop when bottom edge of strip is no longer on crosswise cut (strips are easiest to join when their ends are on crosswise grain of fabric). Cut along lines.

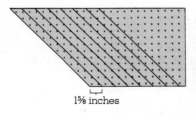

1⅝ inches

3. Join strips. With right sides together, place two strips at a right angle, offset slightly as shown, and join with a ¼-inch seam; press seam open. Sew all strips in this manner to make one continuous strip.

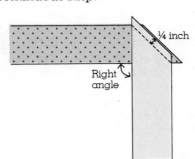

¼ inch

Right angle

Assembling welt

Lay cord along center of wrong side of your bias casing. Fold casing over cord, aligning raw edges.

Set your sewing machine for longest stitch and attach zipper foot. Sew through casing close to cord—but not crowding it, since you'll later want to stitch pillow seams between welt stitching and cord.

With one hand in front and one hand in back of needle, gently stretch bias casing as you sew to help welt lie smoothly in pillow seams.

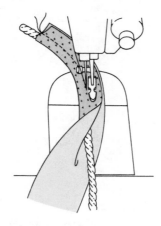

Gathered welt

Welt doesn't always have to look tailored—gathered welt, sometimes called "ruching," softens pillow edges for an elegant special effect. Instead of folding the casing over the cord and stitching as you would for plain welt, you first stitch the empty casing, then thread the cord through and gather the casing to create gathered welt.

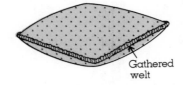

Gathered welt

For best results, use only light or medium-weight fabric for gathered welt; heavier fabrics leave too much bulk in the seams.

The following instructions call for 1⅝-inch-wide bias casing and ¼-inch-thick cord. If your cord is a different size, experiment to determine the necessary bias casing width and seam allowance.

1. Prepare bias strips. You will need bias casing 2½ to 4 times the length of the cord; experiment to see how much fullness looks good with your fabric. See "Cutting continuous bias casing," page 10, or "Cutting separate bias strips," at left, to prepare bias casing.

2. Stitch bias casing. Fold bias casing lengthwise, wrong sides together and raw edges aligned. With machine set on longest stitch, machine baste through casing ⅜ inch from raw edges.

3. Gather welt. Tape one end of cord to prevent fraying. Attach small safety pin at taped end and thread cord through empty casing, distributing gathers evenly. Pin or stitch other end of cord as it reaches end of casing to keep it from pulling through.

Gathered welt

4. Baste welt to pillow piece. See "Knife-edge pillow with welt," steps 2–4, pages 17–18, to machine baste welt to pillow piece, turn corners, and join welt ends. If pillow piece gathers up as you sew gathered welt to it, stop stitching occasionally and smooth the seam.

Zippers & handstitches

Should you bother to sew a zipper in your pillow, or simply stitch it closed? That depends—on how your pillow cover will be constructed and how often you'll remove it for cleaning.

For a pillow that will get a lot of use, taking the time to add a zipper will save you much undoing and restitching later on. On the other hand, if you're making a strictly decorative pillow or one out of lightweight fabric, you're better off stitching the opening closed. Also, zippers just aren't suitable for some pillow styles, as you'll see in specific projects.

Another possible closure is self-gripping nylon fastener tape. While it's simple to use, we don't recommend it because you will not get a smooth, snug closure.

Following are instructions for three kinds of zippers—centered, lapped in a plain seam, and lapped in a welted seam—as well as handstitches for closures.

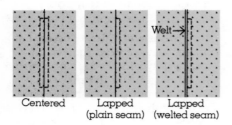

Centered Lapped (plain seam) Lapped (welted seam)

Zippers are available in packages and, in upholstery supply shops and some fabric stores, by the inch from a continuous roll.

If you buy a zipper from a roll, it should be 1 inch longer than the zipper opening so you'll have enough tape to stitch across at top and bottom. One-half inch from the bottom, handstitch across the teeth to make a zipper stop.

If you want to use a packaged zipper but can't get the correct length, buy one that's at least 1 inch longer; then, at the bottom, handstitch across the teeth at the proper length and cut off the excess ½ inch below.

Centered zipper

On a square or rectangular boxed pillow, a zipper centered in the back boxing strip works best. The zipper should be equal to the *finished length* of the pillow's back edge plus 3 inches so the zipper will extend around each back corner. On a round boxed cushion, the zipper should be a third of the *finished circumference*.

1. **Prepare zipper seam.** Fold back boxing strip in half lengthwise, right sides together, and press fold. Using ¾-inch seam allowance, stitch and backstitch along folded edge for first and last ¾ inch; machine baste, using longest stitch setting, for length of zipper opening. Cut along fold and press seam open.

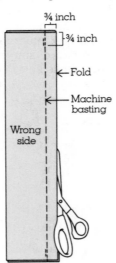

¾ inch
¾ inch
Fold
Machine basting
Wrong side

2. **Baste zipper.** Attach zipper foot. With boxing strip to the left and right-hand seam allowance extended, lay one side of open zipper face down on extended seam allowance so teeth are against center seam. Machine baste the length of zipper through zipper tape and seam allowance only, stitching ¼ inch from teeth (or following zipper tape stitching guide).

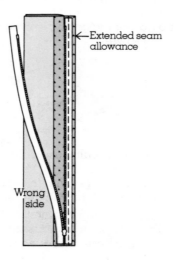

Extended seam allowance
Wrong side

3. **Stitch zipper.** Open boxing strip, close zipper, and smooth it over pressed seam. Pin or baste unstitched zipper tape through all thicknesses. With machine set on regular-length stitch, begin at top next to zipper tab and stitch zipper tape ¼ inch from teeth (or following zipper tape stitching guide). Continue stitching across zipper below stop, up the other side, and across the top. Backstitch at beginning and end. Remove center basting; open zipper several inches.

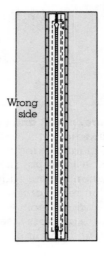

Wrong side

Lapped zipper in pillow bottom or unwelted edge

For any knife-edge pillow or for bolsters, the zipper may be lapped in one seam. Or you may prefer to install a lapped zipper across the center of the bottom pillow piece—an especially good method for a pillow whose top will always be up. In the latter case, *be sure to add 1½ inches to the bottom pillow piece in the appropriate dimension to allow for two ¾-inch zipper seam allowances*. Fold piece in half in the direction zipper will go; cut along fold to make two bottom pieces.

Regardless of placement, use a zipper 2 to 3 inches shorter than the *finished length* of the pillow edge where it will go. On mock-box, soft-box, butterfly-corner, or Turkish-corner pillows, remember that the finished length is the length of the edge *after* you've formed the corners.

For a standard 36-inch-long bolster, either use a zipper sold by the inch or install two shorter zippers so the zipper tabs meet at the midpoint of the lengthwise seam.

1. Prepare zipper seam.

Whether you're putting a lapped zipper in an edge or in the center of the bottom piece, zipper should be centered lengthwise in seam. Subtract length of zipper from *cut length* of seam or edge; divide this remainder by 2 to determine length of short seams above and below zipper opening. For example, a knife-edge pillow that will be 14 inches square when finished will have a cut size of 15 by 15 inches. The zipper should be 12 inches; short seams above and below the opening should be 1½ inches long ($15 - 12 \div 2 = 1½$).

With right sides facing and raw edges even, pin together edges where zipper will go. Stitch and backstitch short seams above and below zipper opening, using ¾-inch seam allowance; machine baste length of zipper opening. Press seam open.

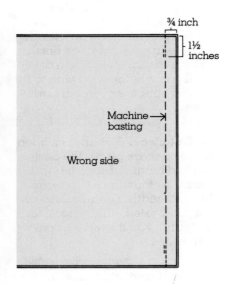

2. Baste zipper.

Attach zipper foot. With pillow pieces (right sides together) on the left and one seam allowance extended (top pillow piece underneath if zipper is going in edge), lay one side of open zipper face down on extended seam allowance, with teeth on center seam line; zipper tab and stop should be at points where basting begins and ends. Machine baste ¼ inch from teeth (or following zipper tape stitching guide) the length of zipper through zipper tape and seam allowance only.

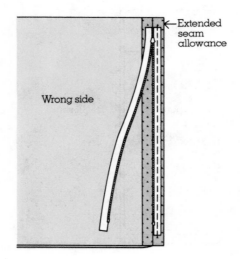

3. Stitch zipper.

Shift zipper foot to other side of needle. Close zipper, turn it face up, and smooth fabric away from zipper. With machine set on regular-length stitch, sew along narrow fold between center seam and zipper teeth.

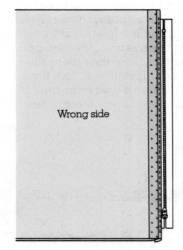

Open pillow pieces, turn zipper face down, and pin or baste unstitched zipper tape through all thicknesses. On right or wrong side, ¼ inch from zipper teeth (or follow zipper tape stitching guide), stitch across zipper below stop, up the side, and across top. Backstitch at beginning and end. If stitching from right side, check to be sure stitches catch zipper tape. (On a bolster, you will actually be stitching inside the tube when you stitch zipper. To do so, simply shift fabric at opening to expose zipper as you stitch down its length.) Remove basting; open zipper several inches.

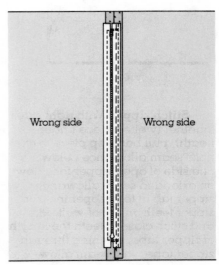

Lapped zipper in welted edge

With welt in a pillow's edge, it's necessary to stitch the zipper differently. If the zipper is basted and stitched carefully, the teeth will be concealed beneath the welt. Remember to use a zipper 2 to 3 inches shorter than the *finished length* of the pillow edge.

1. Prepare zipper seam.

See "Lapped zipper in pillow bottom or unwelted edge," step 1, first paragraph, to prepare zipper seam. Temporarily fold out creased edge on bottom piece. With right sides together, pin top and bottom pieces along edge where zipper will go. Stitch and backstitch above and below zipper opening, using 3/4-inch seam allowance.

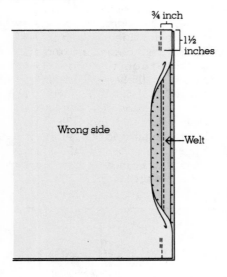

Wrong side

¾ inch

1½ inches

Welt

2. Stitch zipper. With right sides together (welted piece underneath), pull back top piece to expose seam allowance below. Lay one side of open zipper face down on extended seam allowance, zipper tab at top of opening and zipper teeth *on top of* welt. Pin and stitch close to teeth the length of zipper tape, stitching through zipper tape, welt seam allowances, and pillow seam allowances only.

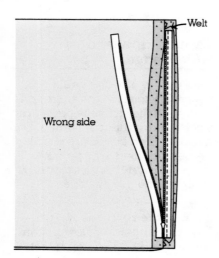

Welt

Wrong side

Open pieces so right sides are up. (Zipper is now attached on one side, below welt.) Close zipper and lay creased edge over teeth. Pin or baste through all

thicknesses. On right or wrong side, ¼ inch from zipper teeth (or follow zipper tape stitching guide), stitch across zipper at bottom, up the side, and across top. Backstitch at beginning and end. If stitching from right side, check to be sure that stitches catch zipper tape. Remove basting; open zipper several inches.

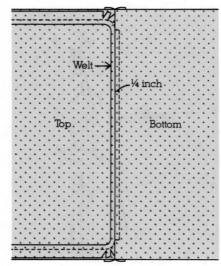

Welt

¼ inch

Top

Bottom

Handstitches

You'll need to know how to do these two basic handstitches to close an inner cover or to stitch together the pressed edges on a pillow cover without a zipper.

Whipstitch is a fast, strong stitch useful for closing the opening of an inner pillow cover. To whipstitch edges, make overcasting stitches about ¼ inch apart. You can close the outer pillow with whipstitching, too, if your fabric has a weave or print that will camouflage the stitches.

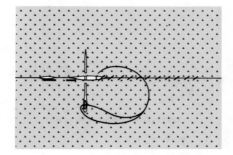

Blindstitch is the stitch to use for an invisible closure on solid-color fabrics. The success of this technique depends on small, evenly spaced stitches.

Slightly fold back the creased edges of opening. Then, working from right to left, take a tiny stitch along one side of one fold. Take the next stitch on the opposite folded edge, a little ahead of the first. Work back and forth, making sure stitches are close and evenly spaced. About every six stitches, pull thread tight, but not so tight that fabric wrinkles. Secure with a few stitches at the end of the opening.

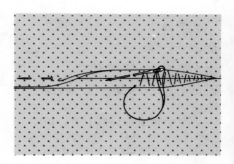

Ties

Your stool or chair pillows will fit more snugly and securely if you add fabric ties to them. Though the ties can be made any width you like, a good average finished width is ⅜ inch; the length depends on whether you plan to tie them in simple knots or in perky bows.

1. Cut piece. To make ties, measure and mark pieces the desired finished length of each tie; width should be four times the desired finished width. For four pairs of ties you'll need eight pieces; for two pairs, you'll need four pieces. Cut pieces.

2. Press and stitch ties. With right side out, fold each piece in half lengthwise and press a crease. Open and fold each raw edge to center crease; press edges. Fold strip lengthwise on first crease, enclosing raw edges. Topstitch close to both long edges.

Fold

3. Attach ties and finish. Place two ties, either side by side or one on top of the other, at corners of pillow top, with one end of each tie aligned with raw edge of pillow piece and the other end directed toward center. Baste within seam allowance. When stitching top and bottom pieces together, check to make sure ties are not caught in seam. To finish ties and prevent raveling, knot ends or overcast raw edges by hand.

Enlarging and transferring patterns

The patterns in the projects chapter are bordered by evenly spaced dots. To use these designs on your own pillows, connect all the dots with horizontal and vertical lines, making a grid of squares over the pattern.

To enlarge the pattern, draw on paper a large grid of squares that equal the indicated grid size, usually 1 inch per square. (Or use 1-inch pattern paper, available in fabric and art supply stores.) Copy the original pattern, one square at a time, onto the large grid to achieve a full-size pattern. For some projects, you will use this enlargement as your pattern for cutting.

For projects such as embroidery, the next step is to transfer the pattern enlargement to your fabric. When you transfer a pattern to a pillow piece, be sure that the design is centered on the fabric or placed according to the instructions.

Probably the most common way to transfer a design is to use dressmaker's carbon paper (dark blue for light fabrics and white or yellow for dark fabrics). With the design on top, place the carbon *face down* between the fabric and the design. Using a sharp pencil or tracing wheel, trace the design onto the fabric. These

carbon paper markings will wash out.

An alternate method is to retrace the design with a transfer pencil onto the *wrong* side of the pattern enlargement, creating a mirror image of the pattern. Then turn the design *face up* on the fabric, with the transfer pencil side *against* the fabric, and press with a warm iron. This image will be permanent, so work carefully.

If your fabric is sheer, you can simply lay the pillow piece over the enlarged pattern (or tape the pattern and fabric on a window) and *lightly* trace the design onto the fabric with a soft lead pencil.

Tufting

It's the little touches like tufting or tying that give your pillow or cushion a custom-made look. In tying, you take several stitches through the pillow (at the center or at equally spaced points), drawing the top and bottom together. Tufting is like tying, except that you sew through two buttons. Either technique will give the pillow a more definite shape and keep the form from shifting.

1. Stitch through buttons and pillow. Using a long needle (preferably an upholstery needle) and strong thread such as button or carpet thread, position first button on top, over tufting point. Take one stitch down through button and pillow, leaving a 3-inch

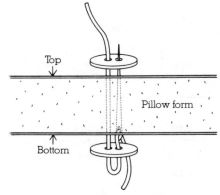

Top

Pillow form

Bottom

length of thread on top. Stitch through second button on bottom, then back up to top through first

button again. Repeat, leaving another 3-inch length of thread on top.

2. Tie end. Tie ends of thread securely on top button or, on a shank button, close to shank. Trim thread ends.

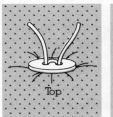
Top

Top

If you've made simple ties without buttons, tie thread ends in a square knot; trim as desired or tie in a bow.

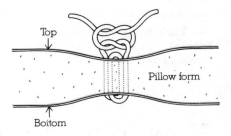

Top

Pillow form

Bottom

Blocking & finishing needlepoint

One of the favorite ways to show off needlepoint is to display it on a pillow or cushion top. But since your finished masterpiece will no doubt be slightly misshapen, before you can stitch it into a pillow or cushion you must block it.

Blocking a small or medium-size needlepoint piece is a fairly simple procedure that you can do yourself. One tip before you block: If you extend your stitches two rows out on all edges, you won't lose any of your actual needlepoint design in the seam allowances when you sew the pillow or cushion pieces together.

Blocking

To block a needlepoint piece, you'll need these: aluminum or copper pushpins or a staple gun, a firm blocking board (an old drawing board or a piece of plywood will do nicely), a sponge, white vinegar, a paper pattern of the canvas, and pliers and C-clamps (both optional).

1. **Prepare work surface.** Fasten paper pattern on board.

If desired, secure board to a table with C-clamps to keep blocking board stable while you're pulling on canvas.

2. **Dampen needlepoint.** With a mixture of 2 tablespoons white vinegar and 1 cup water, sponge both sides of needlepoint until entire piece is damp but not saturated. Vinegar and water help "set" yarn colors.

3. **Tack and stretch needlepoint.** Place needlepoint *face down* on board. Aligning edges

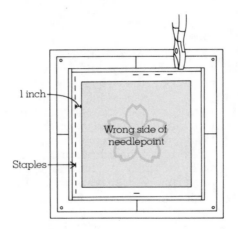

1 inch

Wrong side of needlepoint

Staples

of canvas with paper pattern and tacking or stapling about 1 inch from stitched area, begin tacking at center of each side; work out to corners, stretching needlepoint into shape as you go. For a good grip, you may want to grasp edge of canvas with pliers while pulling it into shape. You'll need to tack about every half-inch or inch to hold canvas securely in place.

Sponge needlepoint again if it has begun to dry.

4. **Dry needlepoint.** In a warm, dry spot, lay blocked needlepoint flat until it is completely dry (24 hours or longer).

Finishing

After blocking, machine stitch twice close to needlepoint edges; trim excess canvas to within ½ inch of desired finished size.

You will probably want to make your needlepoint piece into a knife-edge pillow (see below) or boxed cushion (see page 28). There are several possible edge finishes for both styles; welt (see page 9) in one of the needlepoint colors is most commonly used to accent the edges of needlepoint pillows and cushions. Follow instructions for the appropriate style, treating the needlepoint as the top pillow or cushion piece.

How to make pillows

At first glance, it might appear that the pillows on these and the following pages have little in common—a few taper toward the edges, others have a uniform depth, several are round and gathered. What they share is a similarity in their basic construction, for all are knife-edge pillows, or variations on knife-edge pillows.

The basic knife-edge pillow has identical top and bottom pieces that are sewn together around their perimeter, creating a pillow that's deep at the center and tapered toward the edges.

Variations on this style are also seamed at the edges, but have corners that may be folded, pleated, or gathered, making pillows with the depth of boxed pillows but without a separate boxing strip. (The round sunburst and puff pillows are exceptions.) Any of these styles works well either for a throw pillow or a larger floor pillow.

Before you begin, review "Fabric calculations & cutting," pages 7 and 8. For the how-tos of making your own pillow form, see "Forms & fillers," pages 8 and 9.

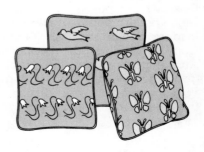

1. **Prepare pillow pieces.** Measure and mark identical top and bottom pieces the *exact size* of the pillow form. If installing a zipper in one pillow edge, add ¼ inch to pillow pieces on zipper edges; for a zipper centered in pillow bottom, add 1½ inches to bottom piece in the appropriate dimension.

Cut two pieces.

A knife-edge pillow, with or without welt, may have exaggerated points at the corners if you cut the pieces exactly square. By

Knife-edge pillow with welt

The simplest pillow to sew, the basic knife-edge pillow, consists of two pieces sewn together. If you add welt or ruffles to the pillow's

perimeter, you will first attach the trim to the top piece and then stitch the pieces together.

The most successful knife-edge pillows are square or rectangular; round ones, unless they have ruffles, tend to pucker at the edges.

tapering the corners just a little as you cut, you can end up with a filled pillow that will appear to be square. Don't automatically taper the corners on all pillows, though; on fabrics with large, distinct patterns, tapering the corners may distort the pattern.

To taper corners, measure and mark points ½ inch from each corner along raw edges. Also measure from each corner and mark points at a distance equal to one-fourth the side length. Connect these side points with the ½-inch points on opposite corners; cut along these lines.

To measure, mark, and cut ruffles, see "Ruffles," step 1, page 27.

If you're making a knife-edge pillow without welt or other edge trim, skip to Step 5.

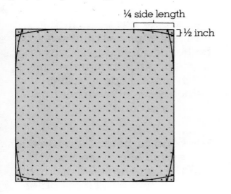

2. Baste welt to top pillow piece.
See "Welt," pages 9–11, to cut bias casing and assemble welt.

Note: When you machine baste welt to top pillow piece, sew *on* welt stitching; when sewing pillow pieces together, stitch seam *between* welt stitching and cord.

If, when you finish basting welt, pillow piece puckers, press wrong side, gently stretching edges.

If installing a zipper, press under ¾-inch seam allowance on both edges where zipper will go; when basting welt along zipper edge, position welt stitching over this crease.

Beginning at midpoint of any edge except zipper edge, lay welt on right side of top pillow piece, welt seam allowances aligned with raw edges of pillow piece. With machine set on longest stitch, using a zipper foot, begin basting 1½ inches from end of welt.

3. Turn corners.
Stitch welt to within 1½ inches of corner. To turn corner easily, make three or more diagonal cuts into welt seam allowance *almost* to stitching.

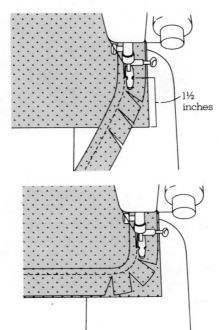

It's simplest to gently curve welt around corner, but if you prefer a squarer corner, continue stitching to within ½ inch of corner. Leaving needle in fabric, raise foot, pivot fabric and welt, lower foot, and stitch down side. Continue stitching along sides and around corners.

4. Join welt ends.
Where welt ends meet, use either of these finishing methods:

To fit ends together, continue sewing around pillow to within 1½ inches of first welt end. Stop stitching, but leave needle in fabric. Cut off second welt end so it will overlap first end by 1 inch. Take out the last inch of stitches from welt casing on second end; pull out and cut off 1 inch of cord. On same end, fold casing under ⅜ inch; lap it around first end. Slip welt back into seam and hold in place as you finish stitching welt to pillow piece.

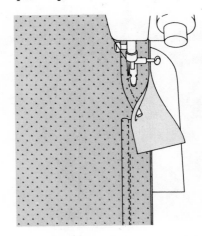

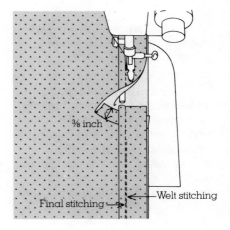

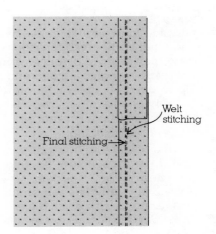

To cross ends, continue sewing around pillow until you get to within 1 inch of first welt end. Stop stitching, but leave needle in fabric. Cut off welt so it will overlap first welt end by 1½ inches. Pull out and cut off ¾ inch of cord from each welt end. With both ends extending into seam allowance, cross empty casing and finish stitching welt to pillow pieces.

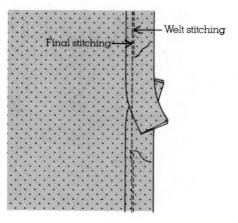

Final stitching

Welt stitching

5. **Install zipper.** For lapped zipper in unwelted or welted pillow, see pages 12–14.

6. **Stitch pillow pieces.** If you added welt, keep welted pillow piece on top; make final stitching between welt stitching and cord.

If pillow opening will be handstitched closed, pin top and bottom pieces with right sides together and raw edges aligned. Leave most of one side open to insert pillow form later.

Begin stitching about 1½ inches above lower corner on open side, and end 1½ inches beyond other corner on open side. Use ½-inch seam allowances and backstitch at beginning and end. Clip corners. On open side, press back unwelted seam allowance(s) to make sharp, straight creases for later handstitching.

On a pillow that has a zipper, turn right sides of pillow together again and, with raw edges aligned, pin and stitch remaining sides, using ½-inch seam allowances. Clip corners. Press seams from wrong side to smooth out any puckers.

7. **Finish pillow.** Turn pillow right side out; if necessary, press edges. Insert pillow form, working corners of form well into pillow corners. Zip closed; or, for stitched closure, pin open edges and handstitch closed (see page 14).

Mock-box pillow

Here's a casual pillow that gives you lots of style for very little effort. As its name implies, the mock-box pillow looks like a boxed cushion, but without the separate boxing strip. The fabric for its boxing area comes from the top and bottom pieces; a short seam across each corner creates a tailored, squared-off look.

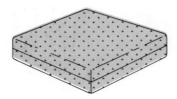

In this method of construction, the mock-box pillow has no welt. If you prefer a similar pillow with welt, see "Soft-box pillow with welt," page 19, or "Butterfly-corner pillow," pages 19–20. Both styles have a boxing area, but the corners are softer and rounder than mock-box corners.

1. **Prepare pillow pieces.** Measure and mark (with pins) identical top and bottom pieces that are the *exact size* of the pillow form; on each of the four edges, add half the finished boxing depth. (For example, a finished pillow form 14 by 14 inches with a 2-inch boxing area requires 16 x 16-inch top and bottom pieces for a pillow without a zipper.) If installing a zipper, add ¼ inch on edges where zipper will go.

Cut two pieces.

2. **Install zipper.** See pages 12–13 to install lapped zipper in unwelted edge.

3. **Stitch pillow pieces.** If pillow opening will be handstitched closed, pin top and bottom pieces together, right sides facing and raw edges aligned. Leave most of one side open to insert pillow form later. On open side, at a distance from one corner that's slightly more than half the finished box-ing depth, begin stitching. Stitch around edges, using ½-inch seam allowances and pivoting at corners. End stitching at same distance beyond other corner on open side. Backstitch at beginning and end. On open edge, press back seam allowances to make sharp, straight creases for handstitching.

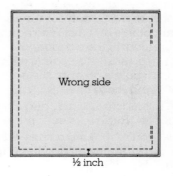

Wrong side

½ inch

If zipper has been installed, turn pillow pieces right sides together again and, with raw edges aligned, pin remaining edges. Stitch around edges, using ½-inch seam allowances and pivoting at corners.

4. **Form corners.** Separate each corner and finger-press seams open. Align one seam on top of the other and pin. From corner point, measure down seamline a distance equal to half the finished boxing depth. At that point, draw a line across the corner perpendicular to the matched seams; length of line should equal finished boxing depth. Stitch along line; tie threads at ends.

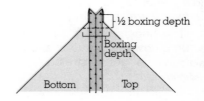

½ boxing depth

Boxing depth

Bottom   Top

5. **Finish pillow.** Turn pillow right side out and insert pillow form, working corners of form well into pillow corners. Zip closed; or, for stitched closure, pin open edges together and hand-stitch closed (see page 14).

Soft-box pillow with welt

The corners on a soft-box pillow resemble those of the mock-box, except that they're not completely stitched closed. Instead of joining the top and bottom pieces and then forming corners as you do on a mock-box, you first make soft-box corners and then stitch the pieces together. This method allows you to add welt.

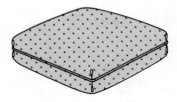

1. **Prepare pillow pieces.** See "Mock-box pillow," step 1, page 18, to prepare pieces.

With pieces together, measure in from each corner along raw edges half the finished boxing depth, plus ½ inch for seam allowance. If installing a zipper, add ¼ inch to this distance on both edges above and below zipper. Mark these points on both pieces and connect them with a diagonal line across each corner.

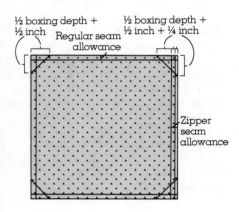

½ boxing depth + ½ inch
½ boxing depth + ½ inch + ¼ inch
Regular seam allowance
Zipper seam allowance

2. **Form corners.** Separate pieces. At one corner on one piece, fold right sides together to form point (exclude extra ¼ inch on zipper seam allowances, if any); diagonal line, when folded over itself, should line up. Place

one pin perpendicular to cut edge and ending at mark. Fold out triangular piece so point of corner is centered over and extends beyond pin. Baste pleat in place ½ inch from edge. Remove pin. Repeat at other corners—eight in all.

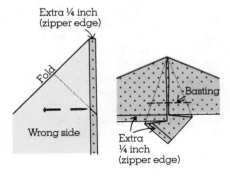

Extra ¼ inch (zipper edge)
Fold
Wrong side
Basting
Extra ¼ inch (zipper edge)

3. **Baste welt to top pillow piece.** To attach welt, see "Knife-edge pillow with welt," steps 2–4, pages 17–18.

4. **Install zipper.** See pages 13–14 to install lapped zipper in welted edge.

5. **Stitch pillow pieces and finish.** See "Knife-edge pillow with welt," steps 6 and 7, page 18, to stitch and finish pillow. When pinning, carefully match soft-box corners.

Butterfly-corner pillow

Similar to but less tailored than the soft-box, this pillow style gets its name from the soft, unstructured corners that resemble butterfly wings. The corners are trimmed diagonally and then folded into inverted pleats.

1. **Prepare pillow pieces.** See "Mock-box pillow," step 1, page 18, to measure, mark, and cut pieces.

With pieces together, measure in from each corner along raw edges half the finished boxing depth. If installing a zipper, add ¼ inch to this distance on both edges above and below zipper edge. Mark these points and connect them with a diagonal line. With pieces together, cut along lines at all four corners. Fold to find midpoints along diagonal lines (exclude extra ¼ inch on zipper seam allowances, if any); mark these points on each piece with pins placed perpendicular to diagonal edges.

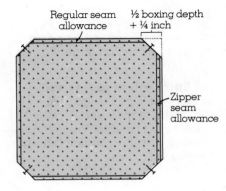

Regular seam allowance
½ boxing depth + ¼ inch
Zipper seam allowance

2. **Form corners.** Separate pieces. With right side of one piece up, at each diagonal cut make two folds that meet at center pin (exclude extra ¼ inch on zipper seam allowances, if any). Baste folds in place ½ inch from edge. Repeat at other corners— eight in all.

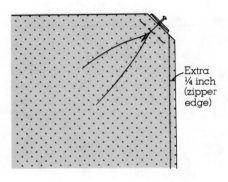

Extra ¼ inch (zipper edge)

(Continued on next page)

3. **Baste welt to top pillow piece.** To attach welt, see "Knife-edge pillow with welt," steps 2–4, pages 17–18. Carefully curve welt around pleated corners.

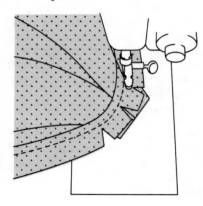

4. **Install zipper.** See pages 12–14 to install lapped zipper in unwelted or welted edge.

5. **Stitch pillow pieces and finish.** See "Knife-edge pillow with welt," steps 6 and 7, page 18, to stitch and finish pillow. When pinning, carefully match butterfly corners.

Turkish-corner pillow

Sometimes called a gathered-corner pillow, this exotic style lends itself to sophisticated fabrics and looks great either as a large floor pillow or as a small throw pillow. Make it with or without welt.

No-welt Turkish-corner pillow

Without welt, a Turkish-corner pillow is a snap to make. You stitch top and bottom pieces together as you would for a plain knife-edge pillow, then gather, wrap, and secure the corners from the wrong side.

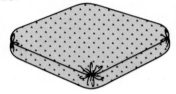

1. **Prepare and stitch pillow pieces.** See "Mock-box pillow," steps 1–3, page 18, to prepare pieces, install zipper (if desired), and stitch pieces together.

2. **Form corners.** Starting at one corner, measure from corner stitching along each seamline half the finished boxing depth. Mark these points on fabric edges. Repeat on remaining corners. Use a compass, a small bowl, or a pencil tied to string to make a curved line connecting marks on both top and bottom pieces—eight curved lines in all.

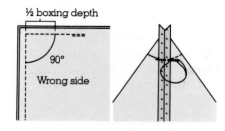

½ boxing depth
90°
Wrong side

Put one hand in the pillow cover and up into one corner "cone." With the other hand, run a small gathering stitch (using strong, doubled thread) around the circle formed by the curved lines on the two pieces. Finger-press seams open as you come to them.

Once you've encircled the corner, pull gathering thread tight, wrap it around gathers several times, and take a few stitches to secure. Cut off extra thread. Repeat at remaining three corners. Do not trim or clip corners.

Wrong side

3. **Finish pillow.** Turn pillow right side out and insert pillow form, working corners of form well into pillow corners.

Zip closed; or, for stitched closure, pin edges together and handstitch closed (see page 14).

Welted Turkish-corner pillow

Adding welt to this pillow takes a little more time because you form the corners separately as on a butterfly-corner pillow before you stitch the pieces together.

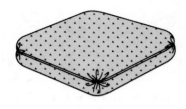

1. **Prepare pillow pieces.** See "Mock-box pillow," step 1, page 18, to measure, mark, and cut pieces.

With pieces together, measure in from one corner along raw edges half the finished boxing depth. If installing a zipper, add ¼ inch to this distance on both edges above and below zipper. Mark these points and use a compass, a small bowl, or a pencil tied to string to make a curved line connecting marks; repeat at other three corners. With pieces still together, cut along lines at all four corners. Fold to find midpoints along curved lines; exclude extra ¼ inch on zipper seam allowances, if any. (See illustration under "Butterfly-corner pillow," step 1, page 19. Lines will be curved, not straight.) Mark these points on both pieces.

2. **Form corners.** Separate pieces. With right side up, hand sew with strong, doubled thread a row of small gathering stitches along curve at one corner, ½ inch from raw edge. Begin and end gathering stitches on seam allowance line (zipper edge has ¾-inch seam allowance). Pull gathering threads fairly tight, but not so tight that gathers overlap; take a few stitches to secure. Repeat at other corners—eight in all.

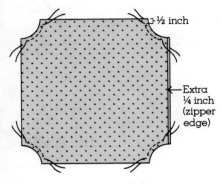

3. Baste welt to top pillow piece. To attach welt, see "Knife-edge pillow with welt," steps 2–4, pages 17–18. Carefully curve welt around gathered corners.

4. Install zipper. See pages 13–14 to install lapped zipper in welted edge. Zipper installation is easier if you first continue seams above and below zipper opening just around gathered corners.

5. Stitch pillow pieces and finish. See "Knife-edge pillow with welt," steps 6 and 7, page 18, to stitch and finish pillow. When pinning, carefully match midpoints on gathered corners.

Sunburst pillow

When made from printed or striped fabrics, this round pillow radiates color and pattern from its gathered centers. Especially striking are sunburst pillows made of border printed fabric.

It couldn't be simpler to make: you sew two separate fabric loops, stitch the loops together along one edge, gather the other edges, and hide the gathers with covered or plain buttons.

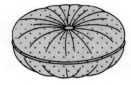

1. Prepare pillow pieces. Measure and mark (with pins) identical top and bottom pieces. Length of each piece should equal circumference of pillow form. (To find circumference, multiply diameter by 3.14.) Width should equal *radius* of pillow form, plus half the finished depth. Cut two pieces.

2. Seam pillow pieces. With right sides together, sew short ends of each piece using ½ inch seam allowance to make two loops of fabric. Press seams open.

3. Baste welt to one loop. See "Welt," pages 9–11, to cut bias casing and assemble welt.

Lay welt on right side of one pillow loop, aligning welt seam allowances with loop raw edges. Stitch along welt stitching, beginning 1½ inches from end of welt. See "Knife-edge pillow with welt," step 4, pages 17–18, to join welt ends.

4. Stitch pillow loops. With right sides together, raw edges aligned, and crosswise seams matched, pin top and bottom loops. Stitch between welt stitching and cord. Turn pillow right side out.

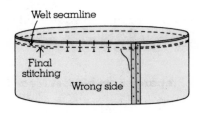

5. Gather pillow centers. On each raw edge, lay strong string, crochet thread, or narrow cord over seamline. Leaving several inches of string free before you begin to stitch, zigzag over string around loop; be careful not to catch string in stitching. Leave several inches of string at end.

Insert pillow form so welt is straight along circumference of form. Gather fabric on top and bottom by pulling string; tie se-

curely at centers, trim ends, and push to the inside.

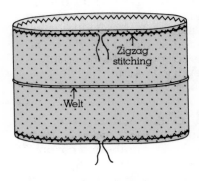

6. Finish pillow. Sew covered or purchased buttons to centers to hide gathers. To tuft with buttons, see page 15.

Puff pillow with welt

You can think of this whimsical pillow as a knife-edge pillow with a small, flat top piece stitched to a much larger, gathered bottom piece. Because of the gathers, only firmly woven light or medium-weight fabrics are appropriate for this style. Since there is no place for a zipper in this pillow, the top piece is handstitched to the gathered bottom piece with the form inside.

You can use a round knife-edge or boxed pillow form; see "Forms & fillers," pages 8–9, for information on ready-made forms and instructions for making your own form.

1. Prepare bottom piece. See "Measuring, marking & cutting," page 7, for instructions on cutting round pieces. It's easiest and most accurate to gather bottom piece around form and then measure, mark, and cut flat top piece to cover it.

(Continued on next page)

If pillow form is knife-edge, measure and mark bottom piece with a diameter equal to form's diameter, plus twice the number of inches you want pillow bottom to come up over top. *If form is boxed,* add twice the boxing depth to this sum. Cut bottom piece.

2. **Gather bottom piece.** See "Ruffles," step 3, page 27, for two methods of gathering bottom piece. Pull strings or threads to begin gathering fabric; then insert form and finish gathering so fabric fits snugly around form. Tie ends securely and trim excess strings or threads; distribute gathers evenly.

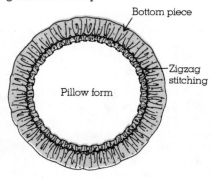

Bottom piece

Zigzag stitching

Pillow form

3. **Prepare top piece.** Following procedure used for round bottom piece, measure and mark top piece with a diameter equal to the distance across top between gathering strings or threads, plus 1 inch. Cut top piece. To help lightweight fabric keep its shape, fuse a circle of iron-on interfacing (with a diameter 1 inch less than diameter of top piece) to wrong side of top piece.

4. **Baste welt to top piece.** See "Welt," pages 9–11, to cut bias casing and assemble welt; welt length should equal circumference of gathered circle, plus 3 inches.

See "Knife-edge pillow with welt," steps 2–4, pages 17–18, to machine baste welt to top piece. Disregard references to zipper. To ease welt around curve of top pillow piece, make diagonal cuts into welt seam allowance *almost* to welt stitching.

5. **Stitch pillow pieces and finish.** On top piece, press seam allowance under. Position top piece over gathered bottom piece so strings or threads are covered. With top edge folded back a little, handstitch top piece to bottom (see page 14).

Pillow shams

A pillow sham is a quick, convenient cover that requires neither a zipper nor handstitching. Because the overlapping bottom pieces make it easy to insert and remove the pillow or pillow form, shams typically cover bed pillows. But a sham closure is also useful for ruffled pillows, where a zipper is difficult to install along the edge.

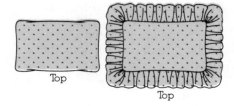

Top

Top

One-piece sham

Think of this pillow sham as one long piece of fabric wrapped lengthwise around the pillow. Because it has only two seams— one along each long edge—this is probably the simplest of all pillow covers to make.

1. **Prepare sham pieces.** Measure and mark one piece. Width of this piece should equal short dimension of pillow or pillow form; length should equal twice the long dimension, plus 5 inches to allow for an overlap on bottom and two double ¼-inch hems on overlapping edges. Cut piece.

Along short edges, turn under ¼ inch and press. Turn under ¼ inch again and press; stitch hem.

2. **Stitch sham.** With right sides together, overlap hemmed edges so sham's length is *1 inch less* than pillow's length. With raw edges

aligned, pin and stitch long edges, using ½-inch seam allowance. To prevent exaggerated points at corners, taper corners slightly. Make sure overlapping hemmed edges are lying flat as you stitch over them. Tie threads.

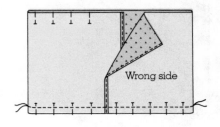

Wrong side

3. **Finish sham.** Turn sham right side out and press edges. Insert pillow through lapped opening.

Three-piece sham

This sham style allows you to trim the edges with welt (see page 9) or ruffles (see page 26).

1. **Prepare sham pieces.** Measure and mark top and bottom pieces. Dimensions of top piece should equal those of pillow or pillow form. Bottom piece should be 7 inches longer than top piece to allow for an overlap on bottom and two double ¼-inch hems on overlapping edges. Cut top and bottom pieces.

Fold bottom piece in half across short side and press a sharp fold; cut along fold. On each of these cut edges, turn under ¼ inch and press. Turn under ¼ inch again and press; stitch hems. To add welt to top piece, see "Knife-edge pillow with welt," steps 2–4, pages 17–18. For a ruffled sham, see "Ruffles," steps 1–4, page 27.

2. **Stitch sham.** With right sides together and raw edges aligned, pin top to overlapping bottom pieces. Stitch around sham edges, using ½-inch seam allowance. If pillow is welted, stitch between welt stitching and cord. If pillow is ruffled, check to see that gathers aren't caught in seamline as you stitch. Make sure overlapping hemmed edges are lying

flat as you stitch over them. Tie threads.

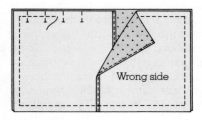

Wrong side

3. **Finish sham.** Turn sham right side out and press edges. Insert pillow through lapped opening.

Flanges

A flange is a flat border, usually 2 to 4 inches deep, that surrounds and frames a pillow. Cut as part of the top and bottom pieces, the flange may be plain (seamed at the outer edges) or open (each piece folded under itself). To add further interest to an open flange, you can include a contrasting strip of fabric between the pieces.

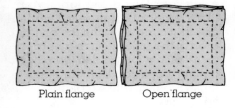

Plain flange   Open flange

Following are methods for making plain and open flanges with stitched closures. Whatever style you make, choose a firmly woven fabric so that the flange has some body.

To make your own pillow form, see "Forms & fillers," pages 8–9. It's important not to fill the pillow form as much as you would for other pillows; if the form is too firmly packed, you'll have trouble topstitching the pillow closed, and the flange may ripple rather than lie flat.

Plain flange with stitched closure

A flange pillow with a stitched closure has the advantage of being identical on top and bot-

tom. However, it is a little tricky to topstitch the flange closed with the pillow form inside; also, when you want to clean the pillow cover, you must take out the handstitching and topstitching to remove the form, then restitch the flange closed.

1. **Prepare pillow pieces.** Measure and mark (with pins) identical top and bottom pieces equal to desired *finished* size of filled pillow (½ inch shorter on each edge than pillow form.) *To each edge,* add *finished* flange depth plus ½ inch for seam allowance. Cut two pieces.

2. **Stitch pillow pieces.** With right sides together and raw edges aligned, pin pillow pieces together. To insert pillow form and finish topstitching flange later, leave an opening on one edge (short edge for rectangular pillow) that's approximately the length of corresponding edge of pillow form. Beginning at open edge, stitch around three edges of pillow, using ½-inch seam allowances; backstitch at beginning and end. Trim corners.

On open edge, press back seam allowances to make sharp, straight creases for later handstitching. Turn pillow cover right side out and press edges.

3. **Topstitch flange.** With either piece up, measure in from edges the desired depth of flange and mark lines with chalk or wax pencil. (Inside these lines, pillow will be filled.) Beginning on a side adjacent to open edge and following lines, topstitch around three sides.

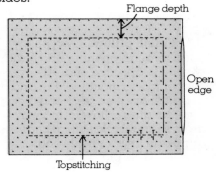

Flange depth

Open edge

Topstitching

4. **Finish pillow.** Insert pillow form through opening and gently work it to opposite end. Attach zipper foot to machine. Pin and topstitch open edge along line, holding pillow form away from seam. Backstitch at beginning and end, or tie threads. Pin outside edges together and handstitch closed (see page 14).

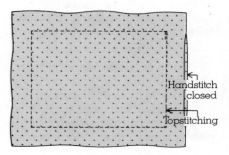

Handstitch closed

Topstitching

Open flange with stitched closure

Instead of being seamed at the outer edges like a plain flange, the top and bottom pieces of an open flange are folded under themselves and caught in the topstitching. The result is a double flange. You can add a touch of contrast by stitching a separate strip of fabric to the top or bottom piece. You then topstitch the pieces together, catching the strip in the stitching.

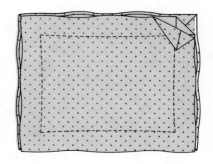

1. **Prepare pillow pieces and optional contrasting strip.** Measure and mark (with pins) identical top and bottom pieces that equal *finished* size of filled pillow (½ inch shorter on each edge than pillow form.) *To each edge,* add twice the *finished* flange depth, plus ½ inch for seam allowance. Cut two pieces.

(Continued on next page)

To make a contrasting insert, measure and mark a strip with a length equal to outer perimeter of *finished* pillow (including flange), plus 2 inches for corner pleats and overlapping ends. Depth of strip should be twice the *finished* flange depth, plus 1 inch. (When you align raw edges and baste strip to one pillow piece, contrasting strip will just peek out between the two open flanges.) Cut strip (you may have to piece fabric to obtain necessary length).

2. Form corners. Working with top and bottom pieces separately, measure in from each corner along edges and mark a distance equal to twice the *finished* flange depth, plus 1 inch. At each corner, fold piece right sides together so marks meet; pin. Draw a line from marks to fold perpendicular to fold and stitch along line. Leaving ¼-inch seam allowances, trim triangular piece. Repeat at other corners—eight corners in all. Turn corners right side out to form points; press corners and folds of flanges so edges are straight and flat.

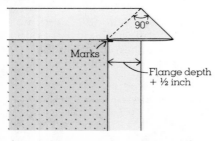

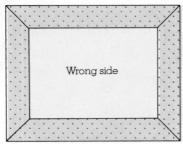

3. Baste contrasting strip. Fold strip in half lengthwise, right side out, and press fold. With one pillow piece wrong side up, measure in from each corner along edges and mark a distance equal to depth of *folded* contrasting strip. Beginning at midpoint of one edge, pin strip to flange, raw edges aligned. At point near corner, turn strip at a 45-degree angle across corner to point on adjacent edge; then turn strip so it aligns with that side; a V-shaped pleat is formed. Pin pleat and continue pinning around pillow. With machine set on longest stitch, begin machine basting 1½ inches from end of strip, and ¾ inch from raw edges; continue basting to within 1½ inches of first end of strip. Cut off strip so it will overlap first end by 1 inch. Fold strip under ⅜ inch and overlap first end ; finish basting. Blindstitch overlapped edges of strip.

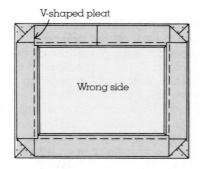

4. Stitch pillow pieces. With right sides out, align corners and outer edges of top and bottom pieces; pin at corners. Measure and mark lines with chalk or wax pencil for flange depth. (Inside these lines, pillow will be filled.) Pin pillow pieces at lines. Leaving one edge open (short edge, for rectangular pillow), and following lines, topstitch around three edges. On open edge ¼ inch outside line, hand baste each flange separately to keep flanges from slipping when you topstitch pillow closed. (If you added contrasting strip, only one flange needs to be basted.)

5. Finish pillow. Insert pillow form through opening and gently work it to opposite end. Attach zipper foot to machine. Pin and topstitch open edge closed along line, holding pillow form away from seam. Backstitch at beginning and end, or tie threads. Remove basting.

Pillow borders

A fabric border with either mitered or square corners can change the size and the entire look of a pillow. If you're making a pillow out of a bold fabric with a dominant motif, a contrasting or complementary fabric border can frame the design. If your pillow top is decorated with a technique such as reverse appliqué, patchwork, or trapunto, a border will enlarge and more effectively show off your work. Even if your pillow is a simple knife-edge or mock-box style, an eye-catching border topstitched to the top piece will enhance the pillow's look.

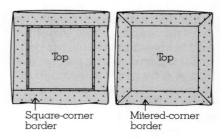

A border need not be just an extension of the pillow top. If you like the look of a flange but want one that contrasts with the center area of the pillow, stitch a border to the pillow top (and to the pillow bottom too, if you like), and then finish the pillow like a plain flanged pillow (see page 23).

The mitered-corner border has four separate strips that are seamed diagonally at the corners. The border can then be stitched to the edges of a knife-edge pillow or topstitched to a mock-box pillow. This technique requires careful measuring and exact stitching. The square-corner border with welt has four strips and straight seams at the corners.

Topstitched mitered-corner border

To add a topstitched mitered-corner border to a knife-edge, mock-box, or flanged pillow, or to a three-piece sham, you first sew the border and then topstitch it to the top piece before stitching the top and bottom pieces together.

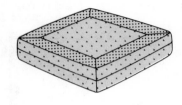

1. Prepare pillow pieces. See step 1 of the appropriate pillow technique to measure, mark, and cut pieces.

2. Prepare border strips. Measure and mark four border strips (eight, if the pillow bottom will also be bordered), each with a depth equal to *finished* border depth, plus 1 inch. Length of each strip should equal *finished* length of corresponding edge of pillow or sham (excluding boxing depth on a mock-box pillow, and flange on a flanged pillow), plus 1 inch. Cut four strips (eight if bottom piece will also be bordered).

3. Stitch border strips. With right sides together and corners and raw edges aligned, pin together two adjacent strips several inches from ends. Fold corner point of top piece to opposite edge to form a true diagonal; press. Unfold, and mark this line. Stitch along line, ending at inside-edge seam allowance. Repeat at other corners. Check before you stitch each one to see that miter is in the right direction. Leaving ½-inch seam allowances, trim triangular pieces. Press seams open. Turn under and press ½-inch seam allowances on inside and outside edges. At outside corners where seam allowances overlap, open and center excess fabric and press for flat, square corners.

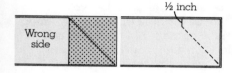

½ inch

Wrong side

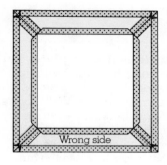

Wrong side

4. Stitch border to piece. Carefully center border on pillow or sham piece. If installing a zipper, remember that zipper edge has ¾-inch seam allowance. Pin and topstitch border to pillow or sham piece along edges.

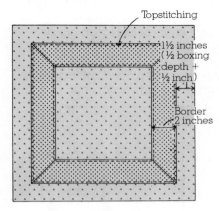

Topstitching

1½ inches (½ boxing depth + ½ inch)

Border 2 inches

5. Finish pillow or sham. Treating this piece with topstitched border as a plain piece, finish pillow or sham, following steps under appropriate technique.

Mitered corner on knife-edge pillow

Mitering the corners of border strips enables you to match motifs or patterns for a picture-frame border. On a knife-edge pillow, you stitch each strip to the top piece and then miter the corners. For this pillow style, we recommend handstitching the pillow closed or installing a lapped zipper in the pillow bottom.

1. Prepare pillow pieces. See "Square-corner border," step 1, page 26, to prepare pillow pieces.

2. Prepare border strips. Measure and mark four border strips, each with a depth equal to *finished* border depth, plus 1 inch. Length of each strip should equal cut length of corresponding pillow edge, plus twice the *finished* border depth. Cut four strips.

3. Stitch border strips to top piece. Mark midpoints on edges of pillow piece and border strips. Working on wrong side of pillow top piece, position each strip on pillow piece, with right sides together and midpoints matching; pin. (Ends of each strip should extend an equal distance beyond pillow edges.) Leaving first and last ½ inch of pillow piece free, stitch each strip to pillow piece, using ½-inch seam allowances. Press seam allowances toward center.

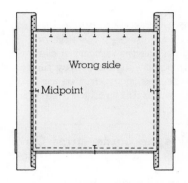

Wrong side

Midpoint

4. Stitch mitered corners. At one corner, pin together ends of adjacent strips, with right sides facing. Mark a diagonal line from point where stitching ends to corner point. Keeping seam allowances free, stitch along this line; trim triangular piece, leaving ½-inch seam allowances, and press this seam open. Repeat at other corners.

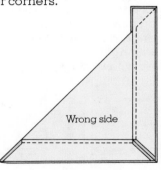

Wrong side

(Continued on next page)

5. **Finish pillow.** See "Knife-edge pillow with welt," steps 2–7, pages 17–18, to finish pillow.

Square-corner border

Choose this border style if you want to define the framed center of the top piece with welt.

1. **Prepare pillow pieces.** To determine what size to cut top pillow piece, you must first decide how deep you want border to be. On a large floor pillow, a 3-inch border is about right; a 14-inch square throw pillow looks good with a 1½ to 3-inch border.

See "Knife-edge pillow with welt," step 1, pages 16–17, to prepare top and bottom pieces, with this change: decrease dimension of each edge of top piece by the *finished* border depth. (If you want the same border on pillow bottom, make that piece the same size as top; repeat the instructions to stitch border to bottom piece.) It's important to cut pillow pieces with perfect right angles, or it will be difficult to stitch a straight border.

2. **Prepare border strips.** On a square-corner border, two longer strips overlap two shorter strips at corners. Consider both fabric pattern and pillow shape when you decide which edges will be bordered with shorter strips and which with longer ones. Measure and mark four border strips (eight if bottom piece will also be bordered). Depth of each strip should equal *finished* border depth, plus 1 inch. If installing a zipper, add ¼ inch to depth of one long strip. Shorter strips should equal *finished* length of their corresponding pillow edges plus 1 inch; longer strips should equal *finished* length of their corresponding pillow edges, plus twice

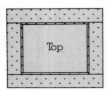 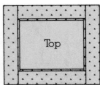

the *finished* border depth, plus 1 inch.

3. **Baste welt to top piece.** You'll need a length of welt equal to perimeter of cut center piece, plus several inches. See "Welt," pages 9–11, to cut bias casing strips and assemble welt. To frame center piece, cut welt into four lengths, each equal to the cut length of edge to which it will be stitched. Remove stitching and cut ¾ inch of cord from each end of casing.

On opposite sides where short border strips will be stitched, with right side of fabric up, align raw edges and pin welt pieces to top piece. Attach zipper foot. With machine set on longest stitch, baste welt pieces to top pillow piece along welt stitching. Repeat on other edges with the remaining two welt pieces, overlapping empty casings at corners.

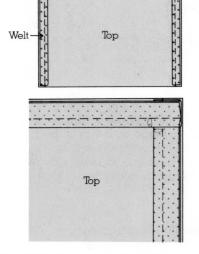

4. **Pin and stitch border strips.** Position short border strips on pillow piece with right sides together and raw edges aligned; pin on wrong side of pillow piece. With machine set on regular-length stitch, sew the length of each strip through all thicknesses, using ½-inch seam allowances and stitching between welt stitching and cord for a snug fit. Fold each strip out so right side is up, and press border close to welt. Repeat with long border strips, stitching

them also to ends of short border strips.

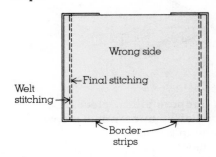

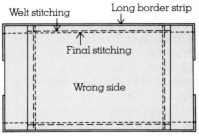

Ruffles

Just as ruffles soften the edges of clothing, they can soften and define the edges of pillows. Adding a simple ruffle can also change the pillow's finished look: try pairing two ruffles (a narrow ruffle on top of a wider one) or attaching a ruffle with welt in the seam.

Let the fabric and the pillow's use determine whether you choose a single thickness hemmed ruffle or a double-thickness self-faced ruffle. If one side of your pillow has decoration that will always be up, consider making a single-thickness ruffle with a hem. If your fabric is soft, attaching a double-thickness ruffle will help the ruffle keep its shape. This is the best ruffle for a pillow whose top and bottom pieces are identical.

Because ruffles are bulky, it's difficult to install a zipper in an edge seam. If one side of the pillow will always be up, you can install a zipper in the bottom piece (see pages 12–13). Two alternatives are to make the pillow with a sham closure (see "Three-piece pillow sham," pages 22–23) or to handstitch the opening closed (see page 14) as you would on a simple knife-edge pillow.

1. **Prepare ruffle strips.** Measure and mark ruffle strips. For a single-thickness hemmed ruffle, depth of strips should equal desired *finished* ruffle depth, plus 1 inch (½ inch for seam allowance and ½ inch for a double ¼-inch hem). For a double-thickness ruffle, depth of strips should equal twice the *finished* ruffle depth, plus 1 inch for seam allowances. When strips are seamed together, total length of strip should be 2½ to 4 times the pillow's perimeter, depending on the weight of the fabric and the fullness you want.

Single-thickness ruffles hem easily when cut on the crosswise grain; double-thickness ruffles are best cut on the lengthwise grain. If you're using plaid or checked fabric, cutting the strips on the bias will produce a different look.

Cut strips. With right sides together, seam short ends, using ½-inch seam allowance, to make one strip; seam ends to make one continuous fabric loop. Press seams open.

2. **Hem or press edge of ruffle loop.** For a single-thickness ruffle, press under ¼ inch on one raw edge; press under ¼ inch again and stitch narrow hem by hand or machine. Or, on right side, topstitch a trim such as narrow lace to one edge. For a double-thickness ruffle, fold loop in half lengthwise, with right sides out, and press fold.

Fold loop in quarters and mark divisions with pins or small marks in seam allowances.

3. **Stitch gathering rows.** To gather lightweight fabric, set machine on longest stitch, reduce upper thread tension, if possible, and make two rows of gathering stitches, one along seamline and the other just within seam allowance. At beginning of each row, take several stitches and backstitch to lock threads for drawing up gathers. Interrupt stitching occasionally—threads are less likely to break and it's easier to gather small sections.

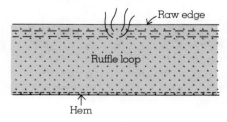

On heavier fabrics, machine stitching may be difficult to gather without breaking threads. Another method is to lay strong string, crochet thread, or narrow cord ⅜ inch from raw edge. Leaving first few inches of string free, zigzag over string around entire loop; stitching should be just wide enough to cover—but not catch—string. Leave several inches of string at end.

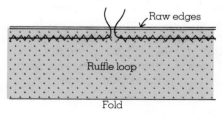

4. **Gather and baste ruffle to top pillow piece.** Gather ruffle by pulling bobbin threads or strings until ruffle loop equals pillow's finished perimeter. Wind end of gathering threads around a pin, or tie ends of string in a bow, so length of loop can be adjusted, if necessary.

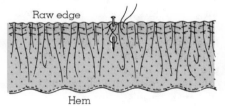

If fabric isn't too bulky, you can apply welt to top pillow piece before basting ruffle. See "Knife-edge pillow with welt," steps 2–4, pages 17–18, to baste welt to pillow piece.

With pins, mark midpoints along edges of top piece; for circular pillow, fold top in fourths and mark. Match corresponding divisions on ruffle loop.

With right sides together and raw edges aligned, pin ruffle to top pillow piece. Distribute gathers evenly, allowing a little extra fullness at corners.

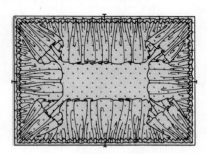

With ruffle up, machine baste around ruffle and pillow piece, using ½-inch seam allowances and pivoting at corners. As you sew, check to see that gathers don't overlap in seamline. If pillow is welted, place stitching snugly against welt cord.

5. **Stitch pillow pieces.** With right sides together and raw edges aligned, pin top and bottom pieces together with ruffle in between. If pillow bottom will have overlapping sham closure (see page 22) or a zipper, pin all the way around edges; if pillow opening will be handstitched, leave most of one edge open to insert pillow form.

With top piece up, stitch around edges, using ½-inch seam allowances. If pillow is welted, stitch between welt stitching and cord. Clip curves on round pillow.

6. **Finish pillow.** Turn pillow right side out and insert pillow form; work corners of form well into pillow corners. For stitched closure, pin edges together and handstitch closed (see page 14).

How to make cushions

When you think of cushions, whether for furniture or for the floor, you probably envision traditional boxed cushions with welt. Structured and tailored-looking, the boxed cushion has an inset boxing strip, usually 2 to 4 inches deep, that is sewn to the top and bottom pieces.

Though the square or rectangular boxed cushion with welt is most typical, you can make a round boxed cushion or soften the cushion's side with shirred (gathered) boxing. Following are basic boxed cushion instructions, with directions for plain and shirred boxing.

Boxed cushion with welt

Before you begin, review "Fabric calculations & cutting," pages 7–8. See "Forms & fillers," pages 8–9, for information on cushion forms.

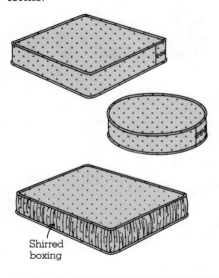

Shirred boxing

1. Prepare cushion pieces.
Measure and mark identical top and bottom pieces that are the *exact size* of the cushion form; if you've wrapped form with batting, measure without pulling tape tight. Cut two pieces.

2. Prepare boxing strips.
If installing a zipper, measure and mark two boxing strips, one for back that will hold zipper and another for front and sides. Length of back strip should equal length of zipper, plus 1½ inches; depth should equal *finished* boxing depth, plus 2½ inches. To determine length of front strip, subtract

cut length of back boxing strip from *finished* perimeter or circumference. Add 6 inches for seam allowances and overlapping folds that conceal zipper tab and stop. Depth of front strip should be equal to *finished* boxing depth, plus 1 inch. Cut front and back strips.

If you prefer a handstitched closure, measure and mark one boxing strip with a depth equal to *finished* boxing depth, plus 1 inch, and a length equal to *finished* perimeter or circumference, plus 1 inch. Cut strip. (You may have to piece fabric to obtain necessary length.)

For shirred boxing, measure and mark one boxing strip with a length equal to 2½ to 4 times the cushion's perimeter or circumference (experiment with fabric scraps to determine how much fullness looks good). Depth should equal *finished* boxing depth, plus 1 inch. Cut strip. (You may have to piece fabric to obtain necessary length.)

3. Baste welt to top piece.
See "Welt," pages 9–11, to cut bias casing and assemble welt. When sewing welt to cushion piece, stitch along welt stitching.

Beginning and ending at center back, lay welt on right side of top piece; align welt seam allowances with raw edges of cushion top piece. With machine set on longest stitch, machine baste welt to top piece, beginning 1½ inches from end of welt. To curve welt smoothly on a round cushion piece, make occasional diagonal cuts into welt seam allowance *almost* to welt stitching.

4. Turn corners.
Stitch welt to within 1½ inches of corner. To turn corner easily, make three or more diagonal cuts into seam allowance *almost* to welt stitching.

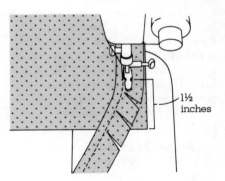

1½ inches

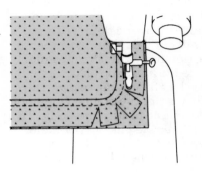

It's simplest to gently curve welt around corner, but if you prefer a squarer corner, continue stitching to ½ inch of corner. Leaving needle in fabric, raise foot, pivot fabric and welt, lower foot, and stitch down side. Continue stitching along sides and around corners.

5. Join welt ends.
See "Knife-edge pillow with welt," step 4, pages 17–18, for two methods of joining welt ends.

6. Baste welt to bottom piece.
Repeat steps 3–5 for bottom piece.

7. Install centered zipper.
For a centered zipper in back boxing strip, see page 12. If boxing strip is shirred, you cannot install a zipper; instead, you will have to handstitch cushion closed on one side.

8. Seam boxing pieces. On a zippered cushion, with right sides together, stitch ends of zippered boxing strip to ends of front boxing strip, using ½-inch seam allowances.

Press seams away from zippered strip. At each seam, fold front boxing strip over back boxing strip so it overlaps back strip by 1 inch (from each joining seam) and conceals zipper tab and stop. Pin overlaps.

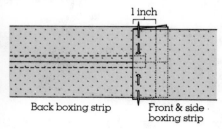

Back boxing strip   Front & side boxing strip

Check to see that perimeter or circumference of boxing strip equals *finished* perimeter or circumference of cushion. If not, adjust overlaps.

Making sure that zipper midpoint will match midpoint of cushion's back edge or curve, divide strip into lengths that correspond to cushion's *finished* dimensions. At these points, clip no more than ⅜ inch into seam allowance along one edge of strip. Clips will help you pin strip evenly to top piece and pivot at corners.

For a round cushion, fold top and bottom pieces in fourths and mark these points at circular edges.

For a handstitched closure, seam short ends of boxing strip (using ½-inch seam allowances) to make one continuous fabric loop. Divide strip into lengths that correspond to cushion's *finished* dimensions. For shirred boxing, divide strip into lengths that proportionately correspond to cushion's dimensions. Clip as above.

9. Shirr boxing strip. For a shirred boxing strip, on wrong side of fabric lay strong string or narrow cord ⅜ inch from one raw edge. Leaving first few inches of string free, zigzag over string around entire strip; stitching should be just wide enough to cover—but not catch—string. Leave several inches of string at end. Gather by pulling both ends of string until strip is desired length; tie ends in a bow so length of loop can be adjusted, if necessary. Repeat on other edge.

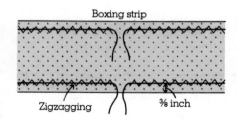

Boxing strip

Zigzagging   ⅜ inch

If your machine does not zigzag, set machine on longest stitch, reduce upper thread tension, if possible, and make two rows of gathering stitches, one along seamline and the other just within seam allowance. At beginning of each row, take several stitches and backstitch to lock threads for drawing up gathers. Interrupt stitching occasionally, as it's easier to gather small sections. Gather by pulling bobbin threads until strip is desired length. Distribute fullness evenly. Wind end of gathering threads around a pin to secure gathers.

10. Stitch boxing strip to top piece. With right sides together and boxing strip on top, match clips in boxing strip to corners or marks on top piece; pin around edges. If boxing is shirred, check to see that gathers don't overlap in seamline.

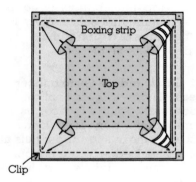

Boxing strip

Top

Clip

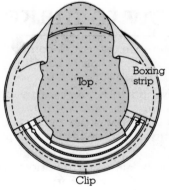

Top   Boxing strip

Clip

Attach zipper foot. Starting at overlap at one end of zipper (if used) and placing stitching between welt stitching and cord, sew around cushion piece and boxing strip. Backstitch at beginning and end. If, near other end of zipper, you find boxing strip is too long, adjust overlap.

When finished, restitch between welt stitching and cord.

11. Stitch boxing strip to bottom piece. On unstitched edge of boxing strip, clip into seam allowance opposite corners or divisions on top piece. Repeat step 9 with boxing strip and bottom piece.

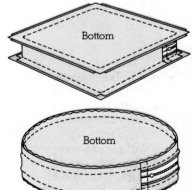

Bottom

Bottom

For a square or rectangular cushion that you will handstitch closed, leave most of one side open (back side, if possible), to insert cushion form later; for a round cushion, leave one-third of the circumference open.

12. Finish cushion. Turn cushion right side out and insert form. Zip closed; or, for stitched closure, pin open edges together and handstitch closed (see page 14).

How to make bolsters

Bolsters are the classic companions to pillows and cushions. While it's true that most bolsters are fairly tailored and firm, there are as many variations in style and size as there are decorating situations.

No matter what its shape, a bolster with end pieces is like a boxed cushion with roles reversed: what were the top and bottom pieces on a cushion become the ends of a bolster; the cushion boxing strip, greatly enlarged, becomes the main piece covering the bolster form.

Following are instructions for making wedge, rectangular, and round bolsters with a variety of end treatments. For information on bolster forms, see "Forms & fillers," pages 8–9.

Wedge or rectangular bolster with welt

Use a bolster with wedge-shaped or rectangular ends on a bed or daybed, or even on the floor against a wall.

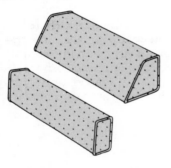

1. Prepare bolster piece. Measure and mark one bolster piece to encircle form; if you've wrapped form with batting, measure without pulling tape tight. Length of piece should equal length of form; width should equal circumference of form, plus ¼ inch on each edge if you plan to install a zipper. (A zipper can be installed easily if you're covering a standard 36-inch-long foam form. On a smaller bolster, you can either handstitch the opening closed, or plan for another lengthwise seam near zipper to allow you to stitch zipper with the one piece split into two flat pieces. If you do the latter, add seam allowances when measuring and marking.)

Cut one piece.

If bolster will be stitched closed, pin lengthwise edges, right sides together and raw edges aligned. Stitch short seams at both ends, leaving most of edge open to insert form. Backstitch at beginning and end of each seam. Along opening, press back seam allowances to make sharp, straight creases for later handstitching.

2. Prepare end pieces. Measure and mark end pieces the same size as ends of form; or place fabric pieces directly over ends and mark perimeters on fabric. Cut two pieces.

3. Baste welt to end pieces. See "Knife-edge pillow with welt," steps 2–4, pages 17–18, to machine baste welt to end pieces. To trim ends with ruffles, see pages 26–27; attach assembled ruffle strips in place of or in addition to welt.

4. Install zipper. See "Lapped zipper in pillow bottom or unwelted edge," pages 12–13, to install a zipper in lengthwise seam. Keep in mind that bolster piece is in the shape of a tube with no "top" or "bottom" piece.

5. Stitch end pieces to bolster piece. On raw edges of bolster piece, mark lengths that correspond to dimensions of each end piece. (To make sure zipper falls at bottom back edge, place bottom back corner of end piece at zipper seam.) With right sides together and one end piece on top, pin corners of end piece to bolster piece, matching marks; pin sides.

(A wedge-shape bolster has a "top" and a "bottom." If your fabric has a directional pattern, check to see that it will run the right way around form.) Stitch around edge, using ½-inch seam allowances and placing stitching between welt stitching and cord. Repeat with other end piece.

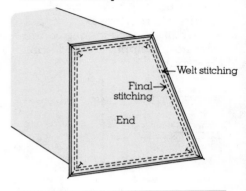

Welt stitching
Final stitching
End

6. Finish bolster. Turn bolster right side out and insert form. Zip closed; or, for stitched closure, pin open edges together and handstitch closed (see page 14).

Round bolster with welt

There are three standard treatments for the ends of a cylindrical bolster—flat, gathered, or pleated. Varying the bolster ends makes all the difference in the finished appearance. A round bolster with flat end pieces looks handsomely tailored, while one with gathered or pleated ends looks soft or sporty. Save the gathered-end treatment for light to medium-weight fabrics—with bulky fabrics, the gathered edges will not meet at the center.

1. Prepare bolster piece. See "Wedge or rectangular bolster with welt," step 1, preceding, to measure, mark, and cut bolster piece.

2. **Prepare end pieces or strips.** For flat end pieces, see step 2, preceding, to measure, mark, and cut pieces equal to diameter of form. Fold these circular pieces in fourths and mark divisions along edges.

For gathered or pleated end pieces, measure and mark two end strips. Length of each strip should equal circumference of form (after it's wrapped, if you are covering a foam form with polyester batting); width should equal half the diameter of form, plus ½ inch (necessary so that gathers or pleats meet at center). Cut two strips.

3. **Seam end strips.** With right sides together and raw edges aligned, seam short ends of strips, using ½-inch seam allowances, to make two fabric loops; press seams open. Fold loops in fourths and mark these divisions.

4. **Baste welt to end loops.** See "Knife-edge pillow with welt," steps 2–4, pages 17–18, to machine baste welt to end pieces or to one edge of each loop. To trim ends with ruffles, see pages 26–27; attach assembled ruffle strips in place of or in addition to welt.

5. **Install zipper.** See "Wedge or rectangular bolster with welt," step 4, preceding, to install zipper.

6. **Stitch end pieces or loops to bolster piece.** Fold bolster piece in fourths at each end and mark divisions along edges.

For gathered ends, see "Ruffles," step 3, page 27, for two methods of stitching gathering rows on one edge on each end loop.

With right sides together and end piece or loop on top, match marks on bolster piece to marks on end piece or loop; pin end piece or loop to bolster piece.

Stitch around edge, using

½-inch seam allowances and placing stitching between welt stitching and cord. Repeat with other end piece or loop.

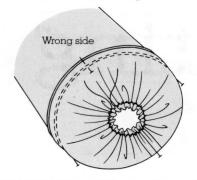

Wrong side

7. **Insert bolster form.** Turn bolster right side out and insert form. Zip closed; or, for stitched closure, pin open edges together and handstitch closed (see page 14).

8. **Finish ends.** For gathered ends, draw strings or threads to gather fabric at center of each end; tie strings or threads securely and push their ends to inside.

For pleated ends, form evenly spaced, overlapping pleats that meet at center of each end. Handstitch to secure.

Stitch large covered or purchased button at center of each end to hide raw edges of gathers or pleats.

Round bolster with tied ends

This simple-to-make bolster is just one piece that's seamed to form a tube, then gathered and tied

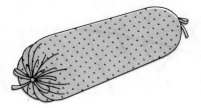

at the ends. No zipper is needed; you just untie an end to slip the form in or out.

1. **Prepare bolster piece.** Measure and mark bolster piece to encircle form and cover ends. Length of piece should equal length of form, plus diameter of form, plus 2 inches; width should equal circumference of form. Cut one piece.

2. **Seam piece.** With right sides together and raw edges aligned, stitch lengthwise seam, using ½-inch seam allowances; press seam open. Turn cylinder right side out.

Wrong side

3. **Stitch casings.** On each end, turn under ¼ inch and press. Turn under ¾ inch more and press; stitch close to inside fold, stitching and backstitching over lengthwise seam. Stitch again close to outside fold. Split lengthwise seam open between these two rows of stitching.

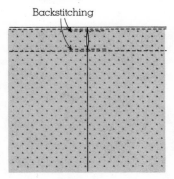

Backstitching

4. **Finish bolster.** Turn bolster right side out and insert form. Attach end of a length of cord or ribbon to safety pin and thread through split seam of casing on each end; gather and tie securely. If gathers do not cover form at ends, untie cord, release gathers, and handstitch or glue a small fabric circle to form; gather and tie ends again.

Pillow Decorating Ideas

Pillows are infectious. One seems to call for two, and two for a whole crowd. Once you see—and lean against—the luxurious effect of even a few of these plump little creations, you'll be putting pillows all over the place.

Sofas and beds, particularly, grow more inviting in direct ratio to the care one takes to pillow them properly. But why stop when you're having fun? A scatter of pillows or cushions instantly boosts the popularity of window seats, wooden benches, and staid wing chairs. Big floor pillows encourage a friendly, casual style of living—including living room picnics and fireside checker games.

So pile on the pillows, the more the merrier. Throughout the next several pages you'll see their colorful and cozy appeal, whether they're placed singly, in pairs, or in haremesque heaps.

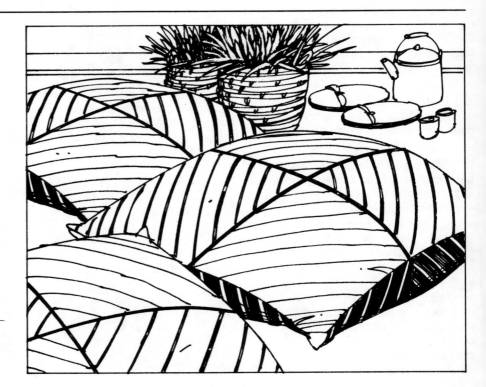

Relax on the floor for a cup of tea, Tokyo-style. These plump pillows will coddle you so thoroughly that you won't want to get up in a hurry.

Sprightly parade of prints against white duck and wicker creates a scene both cheerful and serene. Print throw pillows all have Turkish corners; white cushions are mock-box, round print chair cushion is boxed. Design: Marianne Nicholson.

Ablaze with fiery color themselves, cheery pillows invite you to draw up to the hearth. Their knife-edge corners were cut for a snug fit; fabric ties wrapped around stool legs and tied in bright bows keep the pillows secure. Design: Delsa Ham.

You'll get maximum decorating impact with matched or coordinated collections of pillows.

Elegant blend of pastel blue and white invites you to lean back in delicious languor. Round sunburst pillows add a coquettish touch to the more tailored mock-box collection. Fabric: Souleiado at Pierre Deux.

What window seat would be complete without a friendly cluster of pillows to cuddle against while reading or writing a letter? In the foreground are sunburst pillows, their centers accented with covered buttons. The seat cushion and back pillows both have butterfly corners. Design: Corinne Wiley.

Against a white background, a sprightly pillow medley offers endless rearranging fun. The secret is simple: just collect a number of fabrics that mix beautifully no matter how you design your sofa for the day. Fabric: Marimekko, Inc.

For a colorful, tied-together look, combine prints and solids in pillows and furniture.

Plump pillows, all welted with Turkish corners, contribute to an elegant floral mood. Shirred boxing on *chaise longue* cushion echoes shade's soft gathers. Design: Mary Armstrong.

Welted Turkish-corner pillows emphasize the generous contours of the sofa they decorate. They also repeat colors that play an understated role in the sofa's print. Design: Mary Stiles.

Peppy floral print on one Turkish-corner pillow pairs happily with lustrous blue corduroy. Design: Cannell & Chaffin, Inc.

Interest at the edges comes from stitched pillow borders, flanges, ribbon trims.

Pile up the pillows in a great heap of different sizes, shapes, and decorative detail. Then sink back in comfort for afternoon tea in bed. Design: Mary Joan Sammann.

Natty napkins take naturally to pillows. Flanges on those in the foreground make the most of crisp gingham designs, with nothing lost in seams.

Persian pillow plenitude means at least four in rich Byzantine prints. These graduate elegantly from a pretty round sunburst to a generously proportioned mock-box. Design: Benita McConnell.

Like ornate picture frames, mitered-corner, topstitched borders adorn the fronts of mock-box pillows. Design: Delsa Ham.

School of fish swimming across a window seat began as boldly printed fabric. Solid-color floor pillows accent fishes' tropical brilliance. Design: Corinne Wiley.

If your thumb is green or even faintly minty, you'll appreciate these plant-lover's prizes. Each knife-edge pillow was sewn from a panel of fabric designed for purposes like pillows.

These special pillow pictures
began as distinctive graphic
fabrics.

Geese encircling center of one pillow of this duo were originally meant
to drape a small table. The cloth
came with the matching tea service,
but was chosen instead to decorate
the face of a large, welted and
bordered floor pillow.

Handpainted or printed fabrics become one-of-a-kind pillow masterpieces.

Splashy painted bouquets put pillow artwork right on the sofa where you can lean back against it. White fabric sets off rich colors in these knife-edge styles. Design: Design Concepts.

Series of crisp woodblock prints, each set off with square-corner border, hints that a feathered-friend lover lurks somewhere in this garden. Design: Jean Allen.

Like elegant abstract art, painted silk pillows add muted colors to a creamy beige room. Design: Bob Rogers.

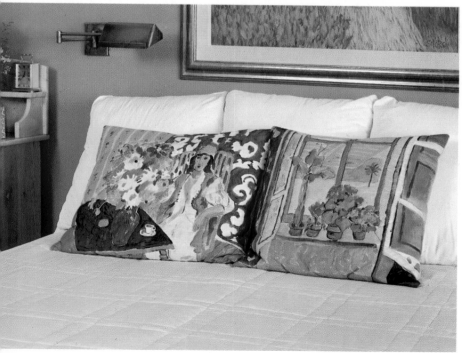

The art of the pillow moves forward with this pair of Matisse-like pillow paintings. Each was painted, outline-quilted, then stitched to make a simple knife-edge pillow. Design: Trudy Craig.

Antimacassars, from daintier days gone by, find a new purpose when stitched to pillow tops. Here, their snowflake intricacy contrasts clearly with dark calico prints. Design: Reo Haynes.

Plush velvet, though one of the fussiest fabrics to machine appliqué, makes pillows of such luxuriant surface that your first impulse may be to stroke them. Design: Susan Kirschner.

Floral center of this knife-edge pillow was appliquéd with fine satin stitching, then bordered with three different fabrics. Design: Susan Jokelson.

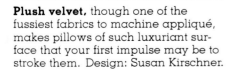

Try old-fashioned techniques like patchwork and appliqué to stitch traditional pillow treasures.

Americana in patchwork pillows creates a very homey setting, especially when combined with rustic antiques near a toasty blaze. Design: Glendora Hutson.

Ruffled shams behind bordered pillows make this collection all the more inviting. Even on an outdoorsy day, it beckons you to lean back and relax awhile. Design: Marianne Nicholson, Barrett Larsen.

Ruffled, flanged, or shirred, grand shams are perfect backdrops for smaller pillows.

Lovely little bolster with gathered and tied ends displays a delicate treasure of lace. Behind, like grand duchesses, sophisticated shams with shirred boxing and deep mitered borders offer plush, royal comfort. Design: Pat Stone.

Like ruffles, simpler flanges soften and frame the contours of a pillow sham, adding to its gentle appeal. Floral bands help to unite bed-dressing fabrics with romantic wallpaper behind. Design: Marianne Nicholson.

Tailored or frilled, versatile
bolsters adapt to a wide range
of decorating situations, both
indoors and out.

While away an hour or two before
you even think about getting
dressed ... you'll have a better time,
wherever you're going. For perfect
whiling away, here is a fresh little
bolster set in front of two ruffled
pillow shams. Design: Marianne
Nicholson, Barrett Larsen.

Coffee and croissants on a window seat—a lovely variation on the breakfast-in-bed tradition. This cozy bolster is a super-simple style made from just one piece of fabric and gathered at each end.

Sun-soaking comfort is assured atop these awning-striped lounge cushions with matching bolsters. The wedge and cylindrical shapes pair for perfect lazy-day lounging as you leaf through a favorite magazine.

Pillow Projects

Sometimes too speedy for the stitcher who relishes a challenge, making pillows becomes more of an adventure when special decorative techniques are brought into play.

On the next several pages, you'll find instructions for a variety of beautiful pillow designs, any one of which could become a work of art to be treasured, whether you keep it at home or give it away.

Gift-wrapped pillows

Wrapped up and tied in delicate double bows, these pillows look like gifts to a friend—or to yourself. A square of ribbon-edged, reversible quilted fabric folds around a knife-edge pillow. You can reverse the outer cover or simply turn the pillow so the bows are hidden. For an entirely different look, make this pair of pillows using solid fabrics and a variety of bright contrasting ribbons.

Gather together...

For two pillows and pillow covers:
1¼ yards reversible quilted fabric
1 yard companion-print fabric
9 yards ⅞-inch-wide ribbon
Two 16-inch (actual size) square pillow forms (see "Forms & fillers," pages 8–9)

Making the pillows

1. Using companion-print fabric, measure and mark four 16-inch square pillow pieces. Cut pieces.

2. To complete pillows, see "Knife-edge pillow with welt," steps 6 and 7, page 18.

Like a gift-wrapped surprise package, each of these beribboned beauties has a square, quilted "overcoat" wrapped around a simple knife-edge pillow.

Making the covers

1. Measure and mark two 22-inch squares of quilted fabric. (These pieces *must* be exactly square, or corners won't meet when you tie bows.) Cut two pieces; overcast edges by hand.

2. Cut ribbon into 8 equal pieces. Fold each piece lengthwise, right sides out; starting at one end, press the fold for 22 inches (unpressed end will form tie). Pin pressed ribbons over raw edges, leaving several inches of first ribbon unpinned as shown; tuck first end of fourth ribbon under fold of first ribbon so raw end is covered. Hand baste ribbons to edges; remove pins. Machine stitch close to edges,

backstitching at tie ends. Check to see that stitching catches both sides of ribbon. Remove basting.

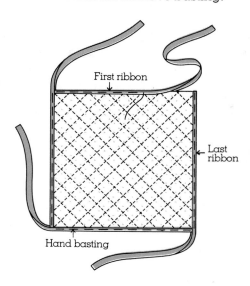

First ribbon

Last ribbon

Hand basting

3. Position each knife-edge pillow over quilted cover so pillow corners are at midpoints of cover edges; draw opposite corners together and tie ribbons in bows.

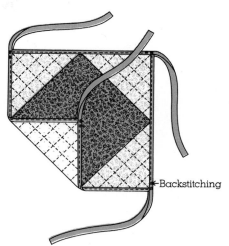

Backstitching

Herbal heirloom pillows

(Pictured on page 55)

"A" is for anise, "B" is for basil, "C" is for camomile tea. The loveliness of nature's herbal gifts is captured here in floss embroidery across the fronts of three exquisite pillows. Save the designs for other uses, too—perhaps old-fashioned samplers to frame. And may your herb garden prosper!

Gather together...

For three pillows:

1¾ yards medium-weight unbleached muslin, at least 36 inches wide, preshrunk and pressed

2 yards *each* gathered off-white eyelet or lace in three different widths

Embroidery floss (6-strand skeins): 6 medium green (MG), 6 dark green (DG), 3 ecru (E), 1 light pink (LP), 1 dark pink (DP), 1 yellow (Y), 1 light orange (LO), 1 dark orange (DO), 1 light brown (LB), 1 dark brown (DB)

10-inch wood embroidery hoop

Embroidery needle

3 pillow forms, one 15 by 20 inches, one 15 by 18½ inches, one 17¼ by 19¼ inches (actual sizes; you will have to make your own—see "Forms & fillers," pages 8–9)

Embroidering the tops

1. From preshrunk muslin, measure and mark the following pillow pieces: 2 pieces 15 by 20 inches (anise), 2 pieces 15 by 18½ inches (basil), 2 pieces 17¼ by 19¼ inches (camomile). Cut 6 pieces.

2. See page 15 to enlarge and transfer patterns to muslin pieces for pillow tops.

3. Divide portions of each skein into three-strand lengths for embroidery. Following color and stitch indications on patterns, embroider three pillow tops. When using satin stitch, slant stitches in the same direction.

4. If necessary, gently wash and line-dry embroidery pieces to remove pattern markings. Place

embroidered pieces, face down, on towel and press lightly.

Making the pillows

1. Beginning 2 inches from end of one length of eyelet, machine baste eyelet to one pillow top, with ruffle pointing to center and eyelet stitching ½ inch from edge of pillow piece. At corners, bunch eyelet a little for extra fullness. Continue basting to within 2 inches of first end.

2. Cut off second end so it will overlap first by ½ inch. With right sides facing, seam ends of eyelet together, using ½-inch seam allowance. Press seam allowance open and then to one side. Trim bottom seam allowance to ⅛ inch. On remaining seam allowance, turn under ¼ inch and press; stitch close to folded edge through all thicknesses. Finish basting eyelet to pillow top. Repeat on other two pillows.

3. See "Ruffles," steps 5 and 6, page 27, to stitch pillow pieces together and finish each pillow.

(Continued on page 52)

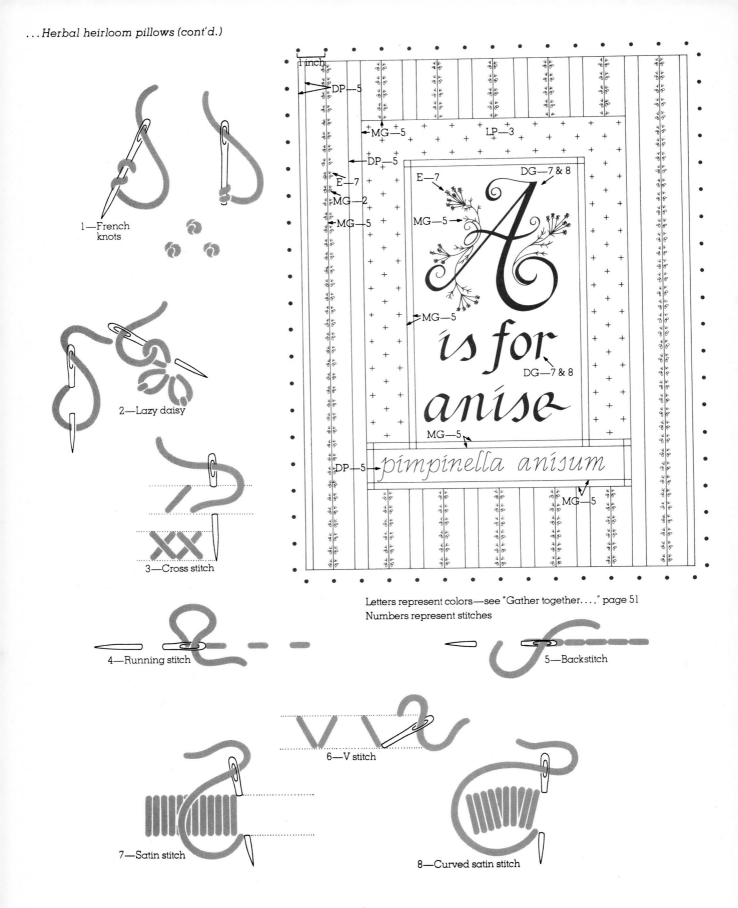

1—French knots

2—Lazy daisy

3—Cross stitch

4—Running stitch

5—Backstitch

6—V stitch

7—Satin stitch

8—Curved satin stitch

1 inch

DP—5

MG—5   LP—3

DP—5

E—7

MG—2

MG—5

E—7   DG—7 & 8

MG—5

A

MG—5

is for

DG—7 & 8

anise

MG—5

DP—5   *pimpinella anisum*

MG—5

Letters represent colors—see "Gather together...," page 51
Numbers represent stitches

Woven ribbon pillow

(Pictured on page 55)

Pretty silk ribbons evoke days of braids, barrettes, and very best dresses. If ribbons still catch your eye whenever you pass a notions counter, let this delightful pillow project give you an excuse for a new collection. All you do is weave lengths of ribbon on a square of cardboard.

Because ribbon widths and colors vary so much, it may be difficult to duplicate the pillow shown. Choose similar colors, or select your own assortment. We don't recommend embroidered ribbons, because they may show through plain ribbons woven over them.

Gather together...

½ yard medium-weight fusible interfacing

½ yard polyester satin for pillow bottom

Approximately 30 yards various width ribbons in 19-inch lengths

3 yards 1½-inch-wide satin ribbon for ruffle

1½ yards welt (ready-made, or make your own—see "Welt," pages 9–11)

14-inch zipper in color to match pillow bottom (optional)

20-inch square of corrugated cardboard

Approximately 3 dozen T-pins or tacks

18-inch (actual size) round pillow form (see "Forms & fillers," pages 8–9)

Medium-weight paper

Weaving the pillow top

1. Measure, mark, and cut 20-inch square of fusible interfacing. Place fusible side up on cardboard square and anchor corners with T-pins or tacks.

2. Cut ribbons into 19-inch lengths. Experiment with ribbons to create a design arrangement of various colors and widths.

Anchor vertical ribbon lengths at top and bottom across interfacing, covering entire surface. Make sure ribbon edges meet and no interfacing shows through.

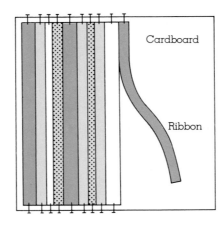

3. After anchoring one end of each, weave remaining ribbon lengths horizontally over and under vertical ribbons; anchor ends. Make sure no interfacing shows through.

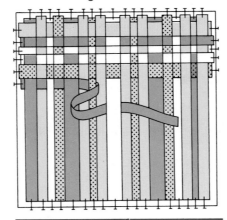

4. Place press cloth over ribbons and, following interfacing instructions, fuse ribbons securely to interfacing. Remove anchor pins and lift piece off cardboard; machine baste piece ½ inch from edges.

5. Using paper, follow instructions for "Round pieces," page 8, to make circular pattern with 18-inch diameter. Pin pattern to woven ribbon piece and cut circle. Machine baste ¼ inch from edge.

Making the pillow

1. Using polyester satin, see "Round pieces," page 8, to measure and mark circular 18-inch-diameter pillow bottom; follow instructions for either plain or zippered bottom. Cut piece.

2. To install zipper, if desired, see "Lapped zipper in pillow bottom or unwelted edge," pages 12–13.

3. See "Knife-edge pillow with welt," steps 2 and 4, pages 17–18, to baste welt to pillow top; begin basting anywhere on circle and disregard references to zipper.

4. With right sides facing, seam ends of ruffle ribbon to make a continuous loop; press seam open and then to one side, as shown. Trim bottom seam allowance to ⅛ inch. Turn under and press edge of top seam allowance ¼ inch; stitch close to folded edge through all thicknesses.

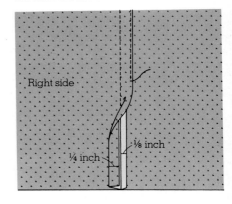

Right side · ⅛ inch · ¼ inch

5. See "Ruffles," steps 3–6, page 27, to gather ruffle, baste it to pillow top, and stitch and finish pillow.

Pristine as a Victorian demoiselle's stitchery sampler, these elegant concoctions honor the herb garden in lustrous calligraphy. You might even tuck a few aromatic sprigs inside each muslin pillow. Design: Karen Cummings. (Instructions on pages 51–53)

Satin ribbons create a shimmery plaid when woven together across the front of a pillow. The finished effect looks deceptively intricate, but the handiwork involved is really quite simple—and great fun if you enjoy blending a range of colors. Design: Barbara Buccarelli and Karen Cummings. (Instructions on page 54)

Let a child design your pillow

For a fresh, whimsical pillow face, consider the kindergartner's point of view. Children's drawings translated into appliqué designs make cheerful pillows that you'll treasure for years—long after the original art gets lost in a sea of paper.

For best results (and out of respect for the artist), don't try to "improve" on your young genius; stay true to shapes and colors used in the original art. Large pictures with simple contours are the easiest to trace accurately and to appliqué. Velvety textures like corduroy will make the pillow as inviting to nestle against as it is to gaze upon.

Gather together...

For one pillow:

A child's drawing

¾ yard off-white fabric of smooth homespun weave

1 yard lightweight fusible interfacing

Scraps of fabric to match colors in drawing

1¾ yards welt in color to match one color in drawing (ready-made, or make your own—see "Welt," pages 9–11)

14-inch off-white zipper (optional)

Thread in colors to match drawing

16-inch (actual size) square pillow form (see "Forms & fillers," pages 8–9)

Making the appliqué

1. Using off-white fabric, measure and mark a 16-inch square for top pillow piece. For stitched closure, measure and mark bottom piece of same size; for zipper centered in bottom, measure and mark bottom piece, 16 by 17½ inches. Cut pieces. Cut 16-inch square of interfacing.

2. With warm iron, fuse interfacing to wrong side of pillow top. Place remaining interfacing over drawing and, with soft-lead pencil, trace shapes. With warm iron, fuse traced interfacing to wrong sides of scraps and cut shapes along outlines.

3. Pin and hand baste shapes to pillow top in positions that match drawing.

To appliqué each piece, thread machine with color to match drawing. Set machine for satin stitch (closely spaced zigzag stitch). To prevent puckering during sewing, stitch with lightweight paper under pillow top (afterward, simply tear paper away).

Appliqué pieces in place, stitching over cut edges. Remove basting. Hand embroider details like animal eyes or a flower center. Press stitching with warm iron.

Making the pillow

1. See "Knife-edge pillow with welt," steps 2–4, pages 17–18, to baste welt to top pillow piece.

2. To install zipper, see "Lapped zipper in pillow bottom or unwelted edge," pages 12–13.

3. See "Knife-edge pillow with welt," steps 6 and 7, page 18, to complete pillow.

Pussycats and romping pachyderm were faithfully copied from children's drawings. Each detail—even clouds, grass, and posies—was translated into a plush fabric appliqué, thickly outlined with zigzag stitching. Design: Susan Kirschner, with help from McKenzie Scott, Tiffany Falahati, and Meghan McArthur.

Ribbon-linked pillow train

This colorful pillow threesome is very likely to become someone's favorite round-the-clock plaything. As a tied-together train, it's great for chugging around the house by day. Then, when bedtime arrives, its separate snuggly pillows are just the right cozy companions for a tired traveler.

We offer patterns for three pillows, but you may want to add a few more ribbon-linked cars in your own designs. For more stability, stitch on another set of ties at each linkage.

Gather together...

For three train pillows:

1 yard firmly woven yellow fabric

Scraps of fabric in red, blue, green, and black

Thread in colors to match scraps

1 yard fusible web

¾ yard green and ⅜ yard *each* red and blue grosgrain ribbon, ½ inch wide

½ yard narrow red braid

Two 9-inch (actual size) square mock-box pillow forms and one 9 by 11-inch (actual size) mock-box pillow form, *each* 2½ inches deep (you will have to make your own—see "Forms & fillers," pages 8–9)

Cozy train pillows double as toys. Easy to appliqué with a zigzag stitch, the train can go on indefinitely—add as many cars as you and Baby desire. Design: Phyllis Dunstan.

Stitching the appliqués

1. Using yellow fabric, measure and mark two 11½ by 13½-inch rectangles for engine pillow and four 11½-inch squares for boxcar and caboose. (You will stitch pillows closed rather than install zippers.) Cut six pieces.

2. See page 15 to enlarge appliqué patterns. Smooth fabric scraps over fusible web (but do not fuse). Pin appliqué pattern pieces to appropriate color fabrics and web; cut appliqué pieces and web pieces together.

3. Center main appliqué pieces, with matching web pieces underneath, on right sides of appropriate pillow tops; add smaller pieces. Overlap appliqué pieces where indicated by broken lines. With warm iron, fuse appliqué pieces to pillow tops. Topstitch red braid to boxcar.

(Continued on page 58)

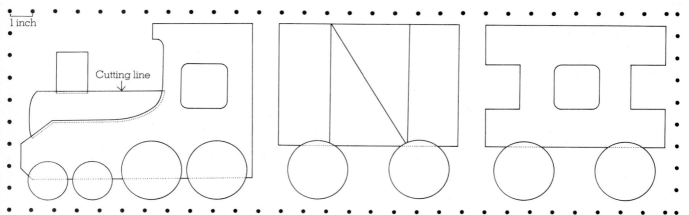

1 inch

Cutting line

4. Thread machine with color to match appliqué piece. Set machine for satin stitch (closely spaced zigzag stitch) and, using medium-width stitch, appliqué pieces in place, stitching over cut edges. For smoother stitches, loosen top thread tension slightly. To prevent puckering during stitching, sew with lightweight paper under pillow top (afterward, simply tear paper away). Press stitching with warm iron.

5. Cut green ribbon in half. Aligning end of ribbon with cut edge of pillow top, baste one piece of green ribbon to right edge of engine pillow top and one to left edge of caboose pillow top. Baste blue ribbon to left edge and red ribbon to right edge of boxcar pillow top.

Making the pillows

1. See "Mock-box pillow," steps 3–5, page 18, to stitch pillow pieces together, form mock-box corners, and finish pillows. On these pillows, half the finished boxing depth equals 1¼ inches.

When stitching, check to see that ends of ribbons point toward centers of pillows and are not caught in seams.

Chrysanthemums stitched in sunny colors meander across rolling fields from one pillow right onto the next. Design: Karen Cummings. (Instructions on facing page)

Crewel landscape pillows

(Pictured on facing page)

Fields thick with flowers spread across this pair of crewel embroidery pillows in a continuing design. Richly textured and colored in harmonizing shades of Persian wool, these pillows are embroidered with two stitches, the satin stitch and the French knot.

Gather together...

For two embroidered pillows:

1 yard natural linen or linen-type fabric, at least 45 inches wide

4½ yards brown welt, (ready-made, or make your own—see "Welt," pages 9–11)

Persian wool (10-yard skeins): 7 skeins medium green (color 1), 5 dark green (color 2), 2 light orange (color 3), 4 medium orange (color 4), 6 dark orange (color 5), 6 red orange (color 6), 5 rust (color 7), 3 yellow

12-inch embroidery hoop

Crewel or embroidery needle

Two 14-inch zippers (optional)

Two 17 by 22-inch (actual size) pillow forms (you will have to make your own—see "Forms & fillers," pages 8–9)

Masking tape

Embroidering the pillows

1. If pillow openings will be handstitched closed, measure and mark four pillow pieces, each 17 by 22 inches; for zippered closures, pieces should be 17 by 22¼ inches. Cut pieces. Bind raw edges with masking tape to prevent raveling.

2. See page 15 to enlarge and transfer patterns to pillow tops. Place each design on fabric so that outside edge of satin stitch border is 2 inches from top and side edges. At bottom edge, the extra distance from satin stitch border to raw edge will make the design appear balanced when the pillow is finished.

3. See page 52 for illustrations of straight and curved satin stitches and French knots. Following color indications on patterns, satin stitch leaves, stems, flowers, and borders; use a combination of straight and curved satin stitches where necessary to fill in areas completely. With yellow or another contrasting color, make a cluster of French knots in center of each flower.

4. With crewel embroidery face down over several towels, lightly press stitching with steam iron, while gently pulling fabric back into shape. Remove masking tape.

Finishing the pillows

1. See "Knife-edge pillow with welt," steps 2–7, pages 17–18, to attach welt, install zippers, if desired, and stitch pillow pieces together.

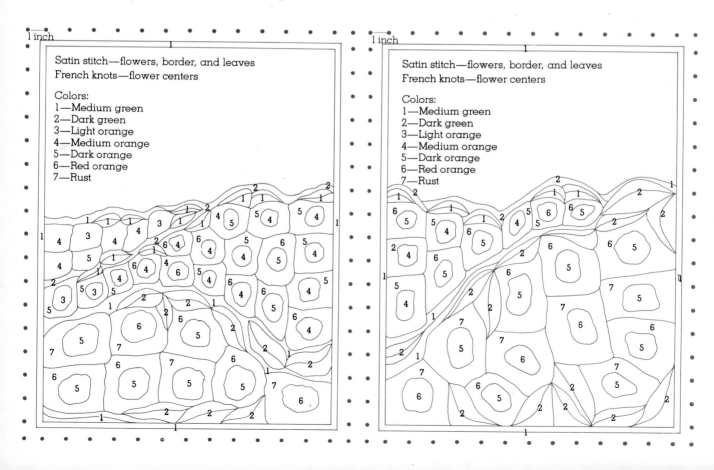

Mola pillow

(Pictured on page 63)

From the Cuna Indians of the San Blas Islands off Panama comes *mola*, a time-consuming but satisfying combination of appliqué and reverse appliqué techniques. To re-create our mola pillow, you begin with multiple layers of fabric, then cut away and whipstitch the layers, one at a time, to expose each color underneath. Details and borders are added to finish the vibrant pillow top.

Gather together...

For one *mola* pillow:

⅜ yard *each* all-cotton fabric in shades of royal blue, orange, gold, turquoise, and dark gold

Cotton scrap, 6 inches square, in bright green

Small cotton scraps in shades of red, pink, and olive green

Thread to match each fabric color

Sharp-point embroidery scissors

12-inch gold zipper (optional)

15-inch (actual size) square pillow form (see "Forms & fillers," pages 8–9)

Making the mola

1. From royal blue fabric, measure and mark a piece 10 by 13 inches. From orange fabric, measure and mark a piece 8 by 10 inches plus two border strips, each 2½ by 15 inches (for zipper in edge, one strip must be 2¾ by 15 inches). From gold fabric measure and mark a piece 9 by 12 inches plus two border strips, each 2½ by 12 inches. From turquoise fabric, measure and mark pieces the same size as gold. Cut pieces.

2. See page 15 to enlarge and transfer pattern; with blue piece right side up, center dog on piece and transfer *solid pattern lines*, *excluding grass tufts* (dotted lines indicate stitching lines for other layers).

3. Lay turquoise piece, right side up, on flat, smooth surface. Over it, center orange piece, also right side up. Center blue piece on top, with pattern lines facing up. Pin layers together inside dog.

4. With tip of scissors, pierce blue fabric only, ⅛ inch *outside* dog outline. Carefully cut dog ⅛ inch outside outline; it may help to measure and mark points ⅛ inch from outline, then connect points to make cutting lines. Set aside surrounding blue background fabric. Turn edge under ⅛ inch all around, clipping corners and curves. Using blue thread and taking small stitches as shown, whipstitch dog to orange layer.

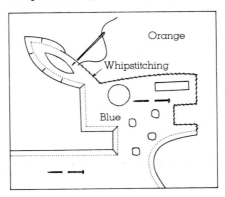

5. With soft lead pencil, draw dog outline on orange fabric ¼ *inch* from whipstitched edge of blue piece. Pierce fabric on pencil line and carefully cut on line; set aside surrounding orange fabric. Turn edge under ⅛ inch and,

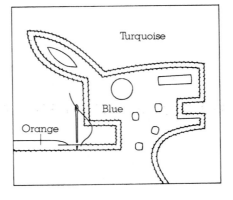

using orange thread, whipstitch orange edge to turquoise piece.

6. Center gold fabric, right side up, over piece and pin at edges and center. With soft lead pencil, outline dog along stitched orange edge (you can feel edge through fabric). Pierce gold fabric on pencil line and carefully cut on line; set aside inner gold piece. Turn edge under ⅛ inch to reveal turquoise and whipstitch gold edge to turquoise piece (cut away gold fabric inside dog's mouth).

7. Place blue background piece in its original position and pin. As in preceding step, press through fabric and outline dog along stitched gold edge. Cut blue fabric on line; turn under edge ⅛ inch to reveal gold outline (clipping where necessary), and whipstitch blue edge to gold piece (cut away fabric at back of dog's neck).

8. Work details, one at a time, in dog's body by cutting blue layer of fabric only, turning edges under, and whipstitching as shown. To work eye, cut away and stitch blue to reveal orange circle; then cut away and stitch smaller circle in orange to reveal turquoise pupil.

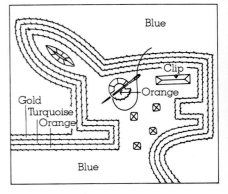

9. Transfer patterns for grass tufts to right side of bright green scrap. Cut tufts ⅛ inch *outside* outline. Pin tufts to orange scraps; cut orange pieces ⅛ inch larger than green pieces.

10. Pin green and orange tufts in position on blue background. Turn green edges under 1/8 inch and whipstitch to orange; repeat on orange, whipstitching to blue. Work inner details.

11. Work background details, one at a time, to reveal gold triangles and oblongs. From assorted fabric scraps, cut inner triangles the same size as solid-line triangles on pattern. Turn edges under 1/8 inch, center, and whipstitch triangles to gold areas. Using blue thread, chain stitch detail down center of tail.

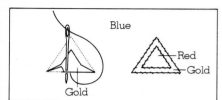

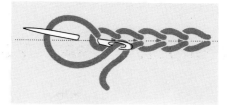

Chain stitch

Making the pillow

1. Press *mola* on wrong side with warm iron. Measure, mark, and trim *mola* to 9 by 12 inches.

2. Pin turquoise border strips to top and bottom edges of *mola*, with right sides facing and raw edges aligned. Stitch, using 1/2-inch seam allowance; press seams toward borders. In the same way, attach gold strips to sides of *mola*, and orange strips to top and bottom.

3. For stitched closure, from deep gold fabric, measure and mark one bottom piece 15 inches square. For zipper in edge, piece should be 15 by 15 1/4 inches; for zipper centered in pillow bottom, piece should be 15 by 16 1/2 inches. Cut piece.

4. See "Lapped zipper in pillow bottom or unwelted edge," pages 12–13, to install zipper in pillow bottom, if desired.

5. See "Knife-edge pillow with welt," steps 6 and 7, page 18, to stitch top and bottom pieces together.

1 inch

Art nouveau pillow

(Pictured on page 63)

Wandering threads, delicate and intertwined, connect floral clusters in this elegant appliqué pillow with sham closure. Inspired by the art nouveau style, our designer chose the ranunculus, a colorfully blossoming plant once used for medicinal purposes, as the flower for her stitchery bouquets.

Gather together...

For one pillow:

1 yard firmly woven rose fabric, at least 45 inches wide

¼ yard *each* firmly woven ivory fabric, white lining fabric, and polyester batting

Fabric scraps in 5 shades of purple/peach colors, plus 1 shade of blue gray

Thread in colors to match fabric scraps, and black

3½ yards black welt (ready-made, or make your own—see "Welt," pages 9–11)

1 skein black embroidery floss

18-inch (actual size) square pillow form (see "Forms & fillers," pages 8–9)

Making the appliqué

1. Measure and mark one piece *each*, 8¾ by 14 inches, from ivory fabric, lining fabric, and polyester batting. Cut pieces. Sandwich batting between two pieces of fabric; machine baste layers together ⅜ inch from edges. Trim batting and lining close to stitching.

2. See page 15 to enlarge pattern and transfer individual flower and leaf shapes to fabric scraps (broken lines indicate where one piece is overlapped by another). Cut 10 flowers from purple/peach fabrics, 7 leaves from blue gray fabric.

3. Arrange and pin flowers and leaves in clusters at top and bottom of ivory piece; hand baste through all thicknesses. Set machine for satin stitch (closely spaced zigzag stitch) and, using contrasting thread, stitch

irregular concentric circles to indicate petals on flowers in full view.

4. Appliqué flowers, stitching over cut edges and varying stitch width. Press stitching (and all appliqué stitching that follows) with warm iron.

5. Appliqué leaves as you did flowers. Indicate center vein in each leaf with line of satin stitching that follows leaf curve and tapers from wide at base to narrow before reaching tip. Pull ends of appliqué threads to back; tie and trim.

6. Transfer curved lines connecting floral clusters from pattern to top piece. Using black thread, satin stitch lines.

7. With three strands of black embroidery floss, make a cluster of French knots in center of each flower. (See page 52 for illustration of French knots.)

Piecing the top

1. With selvages aligned, fold rose fabric lengthwise. Measure and mark short border strip, 6¼ by 14 inches, with longer edge close to and parallel to fold. Adjacent to this, measure and mark long border strip, 3¾ by 19¼ inches. Cut strips from double thickness of fabric (you should have 4 strips in all).

2. To attach welt and border strips to edges of top center piece, see "Square-corner border," steps 3 and 4, page 26.

3. To attach welt to edges of top piece, see "Knife-edge pillow with welt," steps 2–4, pages 17–18.

Piecing the bottom

1. On double thickness of remaining coral fabric (selvages aligned), measure and mark a rectangle, 12¼ by 19¼ inches, using selvages as one long side. Cut pieces from double thickness of fabric. These will be pillow bottom pieces.

From ivory fabric, measure and mark one bottom band piece, 3¾ by 19¼ inches. Cut band.

2. With right side of ivory band facing wrong side of one rose piece (long edge of band aligned with selvage of rose piece), stitch pieces together, using ½-inch seam allowances. Press seam allowances toward band. Press under ½ inch on unstitched edge of ivory band; turn band right side up over rose piece and press. Topstitch close to both edges of band, stitching through band and rose piece. (This band will lap over selvage of other bottom piece.)

Stitching the pillow

1. Place top pillow piece so right side faces up. With right sides facing and raw edges aligned, first place banded bottom piece over half of top piece; over other half, place plain bottom piece so it overlaps banded bottom piece. Pin pieces together. (Once pillow is stitched and turned right side out, banded piece ends up on top.) Stitch around edges, using ½-inch seam allowances and placing stitching between welt stitching and cord. Be sure overlapping edges on pillow bottom pieces are flat as you stitch over them.

2. Turn pillow right side out; insert pillow form through lapped opening.

Hot colors and a flutter of cut-and-stitched detail characterize this *mola* pillow. Design: Charlotte Patera. (Instructions on pages 60–61)

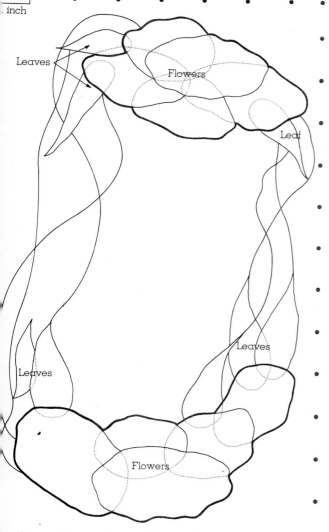

inch

Leaves

Flowers

Leaf

Leaves

Leaves

Flowers

Art nouveau pattern

Languid lines and rich, subtle colors are typical of the art nouveau style, and they are translated here into a lovely machine-appliquéd pillow. Design: Susan Jokelson. (Instructions on page 62)

Summer & winter pillows

With this trio of reversible scenic splendors, you can rearrange the face of your love seat to reflect the changing seasons. The same appliqué pattern, stitched in different color schemes on mock-box pillow tops and bottoms, gives you a double-sided set of pillows. One side wears the cool look of winter, while the other beams the bright smile of summer.

Gather together...

For three pillows:
1⅝ yards muslin
½ yard *each* firmly woven fabric in off-white, lavender, and gray for winter; blue, green, and yellow for summer
Scraps of fabric in navy and rust for tree trunks, light green for trees
Thread in navy for winter tree outlines, gray and off-white for winter ground divisions, rust for summer tree outlines, blue and green for summer ground divisions
3¾ yards fusible web
Three 12-inch yellow or off-white zippers (optional)
Three 16-inch (actual size) square mock-box pillow forms, 2 inches deep (you will have to make your own—see "Forms & fillers," pages 8–9)

Stitching the appliqués

1. Measure and mark six pieces of muslin, each 18½ inches square, for appliqué bases. For pillows with zippered closures, allow extra ¼ inch on one edge of each piece. Cut pieces.

2. See page 15 to enlarge and transfer pattern pieces to paper.

Smooth colored fabric pieces, right side up, over fusible web (but do not fuse). Pin appliqué pattern pieces to fabric and web, turning over first pillow ground and sky pattern pieces for second pillow (mirror image of first). Cut appliqué and web pieces together for pillow tops and bottoms; *allow an extra ⅛ inch on upper long edges of ground pieces* (each edge will overlap piece above when you appliqué).

Place pieces in envelopes marked for each pillow top and bottom.

3. Starting with one pillow top or bottom, lay sky appliqué piece and matching web piece on a muslin square. Place tree trunks so bottom raw edges are aligned with raw edge of sky piece; add tree tops, overlapping them as indicated by broken lines. Make sure outside edges of trees are 2 inches from muslin edge.

Next, place upper ground piece (green or lavender) so its upper edge overlaps bottom of sky piece and tree trunks by ⅛ inch. Continue placing remaining ground pieces so each upper edge overlaps bottom of piece above. Be precise in overlapping edges so that ground and sky pieces will match across pillow tops.

Using press cloth and warm iron, fuse appliqué pieces to muslin.

Repeat on other pillow tops and bottoms for six pieces in all.

4. Thread machine with appropriate thread color for each part of appliqué. Set machine for satin stitch (closely spaced zigzag stitch) and appliqué pieces in place, stitching over cut edges. Reset machine for more open zigzag stitch and sew tree branches. For smoother stitches, loosen top thread tension slightly. To prevent puckering during stitching, sew with lightweight paper under muslin (afterward, simply tear paper away). Press stitching with warm iron.

Finishing the pillows

1. Using triangle or square, measure, mark, and trim each

pillow piece to make an 18-inch square. Set machine on longest stitch and sew ¼ inch from edge around perimeter of each square.

2. With right sides facing and raw edges aligned, pin winter 1 to summer 3, winter 2 to summer 2, and winter 3 to summer 1.

3. To install zippers in edges, if desired, see "Lapped zipper in pillow bottom or unwelted edge," pages 12–13.

4. See "Mock-box pillow," steps 3–5, page 18, to stitch pillow pieces, form mock-box corners, and finish pillows. On these pillows, half the finished boxing depth equals 1 inch.

Shift the panorama of colors, from the cool hues of winter to the vibrance of a summery day, whenever you feel so inclined. Each side of this pillow threesome is machine-appliquéd with the same shapes, but in colors that evoke sharply contrasting moods. Design: Phyllis Dunstan.

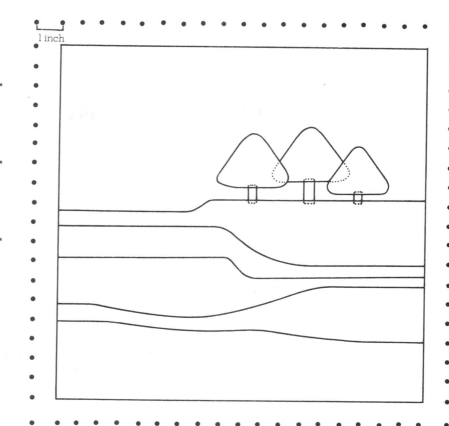

1 inch

Smocked pillow

Though the irresistible dainty smocked dress seems to have largely disappeared from little girls' wardrobes, there is still a breath of life in this sugar and spice tradition. Smocking a pillow top actually requires more patience than sewing skill, especially if you follow the woven pattern of gingham.

Gather together...

For one pillow:

½ yard red/white gingham with ¼-inch checks

½ yard similar weight red fabric

2½ yards flat white eyelet, 3 inches wide

8-inch red zipper (optional)

No. 6 embroidery needle

4 skeins embroidery floss, dark green

12 by 14-inch cardboard rectangle

9⅜ by 11⅞-inch pillow form (you will have to make your own—see "Forms & fillers, pages 8–9)

How to cable stitch

1. From gingham, measure and mark one piece, 14¾ by 32 inches, with unbroken red stripes on long sides and unbroken white stripes on short sides. Cut piece. Use remaining gingham to practice cable stitch, following steps below.

2. Thread needle with all 6 strands of embroidery floss.

3. Each dot on grid below marks position of one stitch. Curved lines indicate whether to hold thread above or below as you take each stitch.

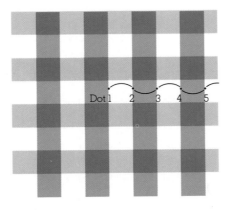

Dot 1 2 3 4 5

Start by bringing needle through, from wrong side, a third of the way down square at row 1, dot 1. With thread held above, as indicated by up-curved line, insert needle to right of dot 2; pick up ⅛ inch of fabric and come up to left of dot 2.

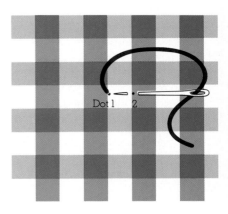

Dot 1 2

4. Gently pull thread straight down, drawing together dots 1 and 2; thread should be firm but not tight, and finished stitch should curve slightly. With thread still held below, as indicated by down-curved line, insert needle to right of dot 3; pick up ⅛ inch of fabric and come up to left of dot 3. Pull thread straight up to draw together dots 2 and 3. Continue alternating stitches.

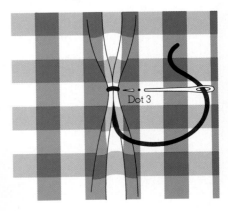

Dot 3

Strawberry-jam colors smile radiantly from the front of this pretty, frilly pillow. Completely transformed by smocking, the fabric is actually plain red-and-white gingham. Design: Mimi Ahern.

Smocking the pillow

1. Machine baste two rows of stitching, one ⅝ inch and the other ¾ inch from each long edge of pillow top piece.

2. On a line parallel to one of basted edges, find starting point (dot 1) for smocking as indicated on grid below. Point should be a third of the way down on inside edge of second vertical red stripe where it intersects second horizontal white stripe. (Throughout project, cable stitches will run along white stripes at the four different positions indicated on grid—a third of the way down from top or up from bottom of a pale red square, or at top or bottom of a pale red square.)

Smock 117 stitches in each row according to grid pattern. After several rows, pin smocked end of fabric to cardboard.

3. When smocking is completed, draw up basting threads so edges equal smocking width.

4. With right side up, pin piece to ironing board cover. Without touching fabric with iron, steam it, rearranging pins and gathers as necessary to make a rectangle with square corners.

Smocked area should measure 9⅜ by 11⅝ inches (size may vary depending on tension of smocking). Include an extra stripe of gingham above first row and below last row of smocking to prevent smocking from being stitched in seams; finished area should now equal 9⅜ by 11⅞. Include additional ½ inch on all edges for seam allowances; trim away excess fabric beyond seam allowances.

Stitching the pillow

1. With right sides together, seam ends of eyelet to make continuous loop; press seam open. See "Ruffles," steps 3 and 4, page 27, to gather and baste eyelet ruffle to pillow top.

2. For stitched closure, from red fabric, measure and mark one bottom piece, 10⅜ by 12⅞ inches (or equal to size of trimmed smocked pillow top). For zippered bottom piece, measure and mark one piece, 10⅜ by 14⅜ inches (or equal to size of trimmed smocked pillow top *plus* 1½ inches on long dimension). Cut piece. See "Lapped zipper in pillow bottom or unwelted edge," pages 12–13, to install zipper in pillow bottom, if desired.

3. See "Knife-edge pillow with welt," steps 6 and 7, page 18, to stitch top and bottom pieces together. On smocked top piece, seamline should run along outside edge of extra red stripes above and below smocking, and along beginning and end of each row at sides.

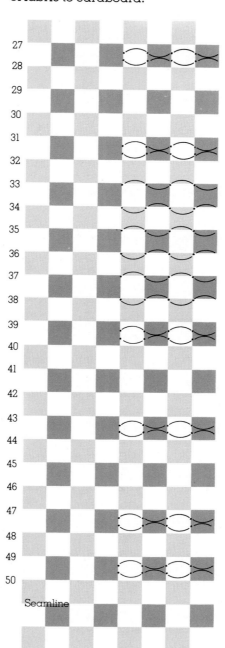

Shiki-buton

(Pictured on page 71)

Casual and versatile, this classic Japanese cushion may be just the answer for your studio apartment, weekend cabin, or youngster's bedroom. Basically a foam sleeping mat made of three hinged cushions, the *shiki-buton* also folds up into a chair or an ottoman; folded, it stores easily in a closet or under a counter.

Foam shops will usually cut pieces to size for you; check the Yellow Pages under "Rubber—Foam and Sponge." Our cushion forms, cut from half a queen-size mattress, were made up into a mat that's comfortable even for adults.

Gather together...

For one *shiki-buton:*

3 yards firmly woven medium-weight solid fabric, such as cotton duck or denim, at least 45 inches wide

2½ yards medium-weight fabric in coordinating print, at least 45 inches wide

3 foam forms, each 26¾ inches by 30 inches by 5 inches (see "Forms & fillers," pages 8–9)

Heavy-duty thread

Masking tape

Stitching the mat

Note: Throughout the project, use heavy-duty thread and backstitch at beginning and end of each seam for strength. All seam allowances are ½ inch.

The illustration, above right, will help you visualize how shiki-buton pieces fit together.

1. From a single thickness of each fabric, measure, mark, and cut pieces according to cutting layout shown at right. Label each piece of fabric on wrong side with masking tape to avoid confusion during assembly. You'll need one 30 by 53-inch panel of each fabric; one 26¾ by 30-inch panel of each; four 6 by 30-inch end strips of solid fabric plus two 6 by 30-inch end strips of print; four 6 by 26¾-inch side strips of solid fabric plus two 6 by 26¾-inch side strips of print; and two 1½ by 30-inch basting strips of solid fabric.

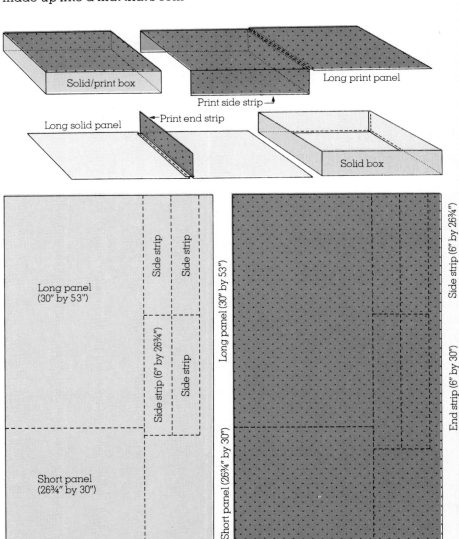

Solid/print box — Long print panel — Print side strip — Print end strip — Long solid panel — Solid box

Long panel (30" by 53")

Side strip

Side strip

Side strip (6" by 26¾")

Side strip

Short panel (26¾" by 30")

End strip (6" by 30")

End strip

End strip

End strip

Solid fabric

Long panel (30" by 53")

Short panel (26¾" by 30")

Side strip (6" by 26¾")

End strip (6" by 30")

Print fabric

2. Construct an open box of solid fabric for one end cushion. Pin two solid side strips to the 26¾-inch edges of short solid panel, right sides facing and raw edges aligned. Stitch, leaving ½ inch free at beginning and end of seams. Sew two solid end strips to remaining edges of panel in the same way, leaving ½ inch free at beginning and end of seams. Press seams toward panel.

Box corners by stitching together edges of adjacent side and end strips, with right sides facing, leaving ½ inch free at beginning and end of seams. Set box aside.

3. Construct another open box, repeating step 2, but this time attaching side and end strips of *solid* fabric to short panel of *print* fabric. Set aside.

4. To attach solid basting strips, fold one strip in half lengthwise, with wrong sides facing; press a crease, then unfold. Fold long solid panel in half crosswise, with right sides facing. Press a crease, then unfold. With wrong sides facing and creases aligned, hand baste the basting strip to panel along crease. Starting ½ inch from edge, machine stitch a parallel line ¼ inch on each side of hand basting, through basting strip and panel; stop stitching ½ inch from opposite edge.

At both ends of the two lines just stitched, make ½-inch-long clips through fabric layers, from edge of fabric to beginning of stitching, as shown. Remove hand basting. Tuck resulting flaps of fabric into channel between stitching lines; secure with a row of closely spaced zigzag stitching. Cut off remaining ½-inch-long tabs at ends.

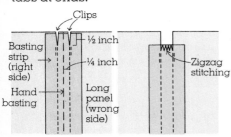

5. Pin a print end strip to one edge of basting strip, with right sides facing and raw edges aligned, as shown. Stitch through all thicknesses ½ inch from raw edge, leaving ½ inch free at beginning and end of seam.

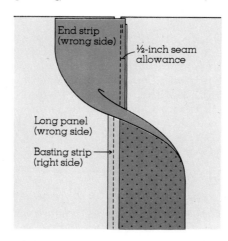

6. Repeat step 4 to join remaining solid basting strip to long *print* panel.

7. Repeat step 5 to attach remaining print end strip to basting strip on long *print* panel.

8. Take up long print panel; to the half with end strip attached to basting strip, pin two print side strips, with right sides facing and raw edges aligned. Stitch, leaving ½ inch free at beginning and end of seams. Press seams toward panel.

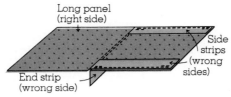

Turn panel wrong side up and box corners by stitching together edges of adjacent side and end strips, with right sides facing, leaving ½ inch free at beginning and end of seams.

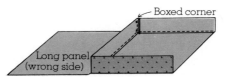

9. Take the partially completed print/solid end cushion set aside in step 3 and the long solid panel used in step 4. Pin one of the cushion's end strips to remaining half of long panel's basting strip, with right sides facing and raw edges aligned. Stitch as in step 5.

Sew one side strip and remaining end strip of this end cushion to corresponding edges of long solid panel, as follows: Pin side and end strips to panel with right sides facing and raw edges aligned. (At this point, cushion will be inside out.) Stitch, leaving ½ inch free at beginning and end of seams. Leave remaining end open to insert foam form. Turn cushion right side out.

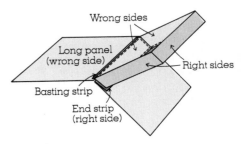

10. To complete other end cushion, repeat step 9, using partially completed *solid* end cushion and long *print* panel.

11. To complete center cushion, take long solid panel with print end strip attached. Pin this end strip to free end of long print panel, with right sides facing and raw edges aligned. Stitch, leaving ½ inch free at beginning and end of seam. Box the two corners as before. Attach one side strip and remaining end strip to panel as in step 9.

12. Insert foam in each cushion, then turn raw edges under ½ inch and handstitch (see page 14) openings closed.

Tube-quilted mat

(Pictured on page 71)

Sun-bathing or sit-ups, yoga or cat naps—pick your own purpose for this colorful, machine-quilted mat of squishy tubes. It's also handy for bedding down an extra child or for guests who always seem to prefer sitting on the floor.

Gather together...

For one mat:

2¼ yards muslin

¼ yard *each* firmly woven medium-weight fabric, such as polished cotton, in 11 harmonizing colors

¾ yard firmly woven medium-weight fabric in another harmonizing color

2 yards firmly woven medium-weight print fabric

3½ yards 50-inch-wide, or 7 yards 31-inch-wide polyester batting (see "Forms & fillers," pages 8–9)

24 by 63-inch foam sheet, 1 inch thick (see "Forms & fillers," pages 8–9)

Quilting the mat

1. From preshrunk muslin, measure and mark a piece 25 by 72 inches (long dimension will draw up to 64 inches after quilting). Cut piece. Starting at one short edge, measure and mark parallel crosswise lines 1½ inches apart.

2. From each of the 11 fabrics, measure, mark, and cut three 3-inch-wide crosswise strips.

From the ¾ yard of fabric, measure, mark, and cut four boxing strips, two 2 by 64 inches and two 2 by 25 inches; you will have to piece fabric to obtain necessary length. Cut remaining fabric into 3-inch-wide crosswise strips. Set aside boxing strips and two 3-inch-wide strips for ties.

3. Choose a color plan for quilted tubes, arranging colors from light to dark, or mixing them.

Using from two to four colors for each band, cut and arrange 3-inch strips for 42 multicolored bands. (You may actually need fewer bands, depending on the puffiness of your batting.) With right sides facing and raw edges aligned, stitch cut strips, using ¼-inch seam allowance, to make 25-inch-long bands. Press seams toward darker fabrics.

4. Measure, mark, and cut 84 strips of batting, each 3 by 25 inches. Lay two strips together for 42 double-layer batting strips.

5. Spread muslin out crosswise on work surface. Lay first band, right side up, at left edge of muslin. Using ¼-inch seam allowance, stitch left edge of first band to muslin.

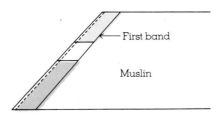

— First band

Muslin

6. Fold one double-layer batting strip in half lengthwise, making four thicknesses. Tuck strip under first band. With right sides facing and long raw edges aligned, pin and stitch a second band to first band, using ¼-inch seam allowance and stitching through muslin backing. (Bands tend to slip, so check frequently as you stitch to see that raw edges are aligned.) Tuck a second folded double-layer batting strip under second band; pin and stitch a third band to second band and muslin backing. Continue attaching remaining bands, checking parallel guidelines often to make sure tubes are straight,

until mat is 64 inches long. Stitch right edge of last band to muslin, using ¼-inch seam allowance.

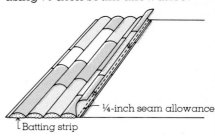

— ¼-inch seam allowance

Batting strip

Stitching the mat

1. With right sides facing, fold each 3-inch tie strip in half lengthwise. Pin and stitch edges together along long edge and across one end, using ¼-inch seam allowance. Turn each tie right side out and press edges.

2. Using print fabric, measure, mark, and cut mat bottom piece 25 by 64 inches. Position ties, one on top of the other, on right side of piece at midpoint of one short edge, with unfinished ends of ties at piece's raw edge. Baste within seam allowance.

3. With right sides facing, stitch one short boxing strip to one long boxing strip, using ½-inch seam allowance; repeat with remaining strips, joining ends to make continuous fabric loop. Press seams open.

With right sides facing and corners matching, pin one raw edge of boxing strip to raw edges of quilted tubes. Stitch boxing strip to quilted piece, using ½-inch seam allowance and pivoting at corners.

4. With right sides facing, pin remaining raw edge of boxing strip to edges of mat bottom. Leaving short edge without ties open, stitch, using ½-inch seam allowance and pivoting at corners. Trim seam allowances, clip corners, and turn mat right side out. Insert foam sheet and handstitch (see page 14) opening closed.

Soft shades of chintz, a dozen in all, intermingle as deliciously as fruit popsicles in this roll-up mat of quilted tubes. A natural for ballet exercises...or perhaps a little flute practice in the garden. Design: Lynn Bilik. (Instructions on page 70)

Three-way foldable cushion comes in handy for lounging, exercising, and even sleeping an overnight guest. You can also arrange the joined sections to make an ottoman or a chair. Called a *shiki-buton*, this Japanese cushion makes an exceedingly versatile furnishing. (Instructions on pages 68–69)

Printed & painted pillows

A potato, a chunk of polystyrene, a stencil brush—what these dissimilar objects have in common is that each is a tool used to print or paint the bright, bold fabrics for these four knife-edge pillows. With the same dyes, each technique produces a slightly different effect.

Gather together...

For four pillows:

2 yards unbleached muslin (do *not* use fabric with permanent-press finish, as it resists penetration and development of dye)

7½ yards off-white welt (ready-made, or make your own—see "Welt," pages 9–11)

Four 12-inch off-white zippers (optional)

Four 16-inch (actual size) square pillow forms (see "Forms & fillers," pages 8–9)

Two colors fabric dye or textile paint suitable for block printing, ¼ pint *each* (do not buy powdered dye that is used for dye baths)

Two ⅜-inch-wide stencil brushes

Potatoes, chunks of firm polystyrene (the kind used for packing)

Soft lead pencil, ruler, old towel or mattress pad, newspapers, and masking tape

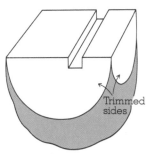

Potato half

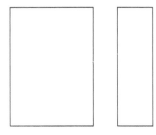

Potato motif

Printing & painting the fabric

1. Wash and dry muslin to remove sizing; press. If pillows will be handstitched closed, measure and mark eight 16-inch square pieces; for zippered closures, pieces should be 16 by 16¼ inches. Cut pieces.

2A. For block prints, use paring knife to cut potato in half crosswise and trim sides to desired dimensions (see pattern and drawing). For areas that you

---

Using muslin as your canvas, and a palette of textile dyes, print or paint your own "designer line" of pillows. Design: Christine Barnes.

don't want printed, incise about ⅛ inch; notch top of potato to make two finger-holds. Trim polystyrene to desired block (see pattern) using serrated knife.

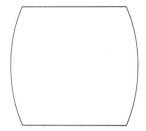

Polystyrene motif

2B. Tape corners of one top piece to padded, newspaper-covered work surface. Measure and, with pencil, lightly mark guidelines at distances equal to height of motif plus ⅛ to ¼ inch.

Using stencil brush, apply thin, even coat of dye or paint to surface of block. Press block firmly onto fabric, lining up top of motif with top guideline. Continue printing across to make first row. On subsequent rows where pattern changes color, rinse and dry block and print with second color for striped effect. Set dye according to package instructions. Print second top piece.

3A. For stripes, measure and mark horizontal guidelines (the stripes in these pillows are ½ and ¾ inch wide, with ¼ inch of white space separating individual stripes and ⅝ inch between groups of stripes).

3B. With stencil brush, paint stripes following guidelines; don't worry about straying outside the boundaries. Set dye according to package instructions. Paint second top piece in other stripe design.

Making the pillows

1. See "Knife-edge pillow with welt," steps 2–7, pages 17–18, to attach welt, install zippers (if desired), and stitch pillow pieces together.

Lemon & orange chair pillow

When art discovers technology, the results are often smashing. Our designer used a color photocopy machine and actual orange and lemon slices to produce a cheerful chair pillow. All you need to copy it are fruit slices or other bright, flat objects, and access to a color copy machine.

Check the Yellow Pages under "Copy & Duplicating Service" for firms that make color copies. Make sure the one you visit has transfer paper and a heat-setting machine to transfer the paper color copy to fabric.

Gather together...

For one chair pillow:
Orange and lemon slices
Firmly woven white fabric in
 length equal to depth of seat
Heavy paper slightly larger than
 seat
½-inch-thick foam form equal to
 size of seat (see "Forms &
 fillers," pages 8–9)
Contrasting welt in length equal
 to seat perimeter plus 3 inches
 (ready-made, or make your
 own—see "Welt," pages 9–11)
Eight 12-inch ties (see pages 14–15)

Making the pattern

1. Lay paper on seat and trim to desired size of finished pillow.

2. Pin paper pattern to double thickness of fabric, allowing at least ½ inch of extra fabric beyond pattern edges.

3. Measure and mark cutting lines ½ inch beyond pattern edges; cut two pieces.

Copying the pillow top

1. With design objects and pillow pieces in hand, visit copy center—technician there will help you make copy (keep objects at least 2 inches from edges).

Making the pillow

1. See "Knife-edge pillow with welt," steps 2–4, pages 17–18, to assemble welt and baste it to top piece.

2. With raw ends of ties at cut edge of pillow piece and loose ends directed toward center, pin and baste two ties, one on top of the other, at each corner.

3. See "Knife-edge pillow with welt," steps 6 and 7, page 18, to stitch pillow, disregarding references to zipper.

Citric celebration of the widely acclaimed vitamin represents only one of many design possibilities for decorating fabrics with a heat-transferred color photocopy. Design: Phyllis Mufson.

Stencil yourself a pillow front, dainty and bright as a Pennsylvania Dutch parlor. The technique is easy and quick: you simply brush textile paint through cut-outs of each motif. Design: Phyllis Mufson. (Instructions on page 75)

Crisp geometric baskets result from careful piecing of triangles and squares. With curved handles toward the center, they compose a symmetrical configuration you might see through a kaleidoscope. Design: Glendora Hutson. (Instructions on pages 76–77)

Early American stencil pillow

(Pictured on page 74)

The American folk art tradition is rich with decorative designs stenciled on floors, furniture, and walls. Here the simple technique of stenciling—painting through a cut-out pattern—is used on fabric, producing a striking pillow top that is then framed and welted in small-dot prints. There's a knack to getting crisp stenciled edges, so before you begin your pillow top, practice the technique on scraps of fabric.

Gather together...

For one stenciled pillow:

½ yard firmly woven white fabric

½ yard firmly woven white-on-brown dotted fabric

1⅞ yards red welt (ready-made, or use white-on-red dotted fabric and make your own—see "Welt," pages 9–11)

14-inch brown zipper (optional)

17-inch (actual size) square pillow form (see "Forms & fillers," pages 8–9)

12-inch square of stencil paper or other heavy paper

⅜-inch-wide stencil brush

Brown and red textile paints

Craft knife or single-edge razor blade

Newspaper and masking tape

Stenciling the design

1. Wash, dry, and press white fabric. Measure and mark a 14-inch square for stenciled pillow top. Cut piece.

2. Tape corners of top piece to newspaper-covered work surface.

3. See page 15 to enlarge and transfer pattern to stencil paper. Lay stencil paper over several layers of newspaper and, using craft knife, cut out areas to be painted. Make cuts smooth, with no jagged edges. Center stencil paper on fabric and tape outside edges to fabric.

4. Dip stencil brush into brown textile paint; dab on newspaper several times to remove excess paint and distribute paint evenly.

5. Holding brush at a 45° angle to fabric and pressing cut edges of design flat against fabric, apply paint to appropriate areas of fabric. Start each stroke on stencil paper near cut edge and brush toward center of exposed area. (Never brush *against* cut edges or paint will seep under paper.)

Repeat with red paint in remaining areas, being careful not to smear brown paint. Carefully untape stencil paper and lift off fabric; allow paint to dry and set according to package instructions.

Making the pillow

1. Using brown dotted fabric, measure and mark four border strips, *each* 17 inches long and 2½ inches deep, and one 17-inch square for pillow bottom. If you plan to install lapped zipper centered in pillow bottom, allow extra 1½ inches on one edge of bottom piece only. Cut pieces.

2. See "Mitered-corner border on knife-edge pillow," steps 3 and 4, page 25, to stitch border to pillow top. See "Knife-edge pillow with welt," steps 2–4, pages 17–18, to baste welt to top piece. To install lapped zipper in pillow bottom, if desired, see pages 12–13. See "Knife-edge pillow with welt," steps 6 and 7, page 18, to stitch pieces and finish pillow.

1 inch

A quartet of patchwork baskets

(Pictured on page 74)

If patchwork is your stitchery cup of tea, this pillow should reward you with hours of sweet solace. But, not *too* many hours. While faithful to the methods of old-fashioned patchwork, making this pillow takes only a fraction of the time our great-grandmothers spent on similar designs. You construct the patchwork by joining four squares, each consisting of a basket and its surrounding area.

Gather together...

For one patchwork pillow:

¼ yard firmly woven small-print fabric for baskets (cotton works best)

¼ yard firmly woven contrasting print fabric for background squares

1⅜ yards decorative border, 1 inch wide (embroidered ribbon or pieces of floral striped fabric)

½ yard firmly woven solid fabric for pillow bottom and borders

2 yards welt to match solid fabric (ready-made, or make your own—see "Welt," pages 9–11)

1 sheet clear acetate (available in art supply stores)

Metal ruler

Craft knife

Fine-point indelible marking pen or sharp, soft lead pencil

16-inch (actual size) square pillow form (see "Forms & fillers," pages 8–9)

12-inch zipper in color to match bottom and borders (optional)

Piecing the patchwork

Note: Seam allowances throughout the patchwork instructions are ¼ inch.

1. Tape acetate sheet over pattern pieces below and, using metal ruler and craft knife, cut a template for each piece *except* curved handle along solid lines.

2. For *each* quarter of the pillow top (one basket and surrounding square area), you'll need two small triangles and one large triangle of basket fabric, plus two large triangles and two squares of background fabric. (Handle is explained in step 3.)

Lay print fabrics wrong side up. Arrange each template with one straight side on lengthwise or crosswise grain; to save fabric and minimize cutting, lay out squares and triangles in pairs that share straight edges. Trace around templates with marking pen. Cut pieces. Keep pieces for each basket and its surrounding area in separate envelopes.

3. On wrong side of basket fabric, trace around handle template four times, leaving 1 inch between handles. Machine baste over traced lines. Cut handle pieces ¼ inch beyond stitching; clip curves close to stitching and press under ¼ inch, using machine basting as guide. Do not turn under handle ends. Carefully remove basting; press edges again.

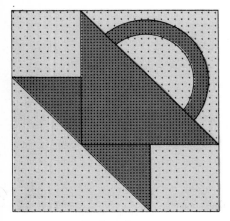

Patchwork square

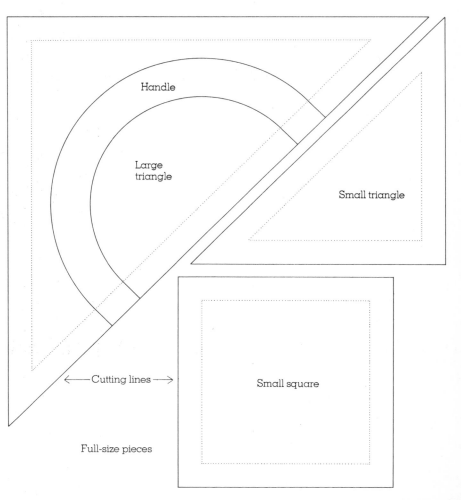

Handle

Large triangle

Small triangle

←— Cutting lines —→

Small square

Full-size pieces

4. From one envelope, remove two small triangles of basket fabric and two squares of background fabric. With right sides together and using ¼-inch seam allowance, stitch a square to each triangle as shown. Press seams toward triangles.

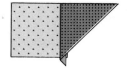

Small square   Small triangle

5. Remove one large triangle of background fabric and place it right side up. Over it, also right side up, place one handle so ends extend ⅛ inch beyond long edge of triangle. Remove large triangle of basket fabric and, with right sides facing and long raw edges aligned, pin it to background triangle with handle. Using ¼-inch seam allowance, stitch along edge, sewing through handle ends. Press seams toward basket triangle; press piece flat. Hand baste handle to background triangle.

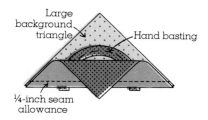

Large background triangle   Hand basting

¼-inch seam allowance

6. With right sides facing and raw edges aligned, stitch pieces finished in step 4 to remaining sides of large basket triangle. Press seams toward large basket triangle; press piece flat.

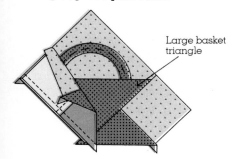

Large basket triangle

7. Remove other large triangle of background fabric. Fold in half, aligning short sides, and crease to mark midpoint of long edge; unfold. Match midpoint to bottom point of large basket triangle. With right sides facing and raw edges aligned, stitch long edges, using ¼-inch seam allowance. Press seams toward background triangle; press piece flat.

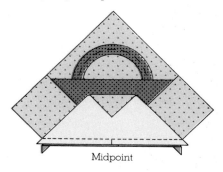

Midpoint

8. Repeat steps 4–7 for remaining three sections of pillow top. With right sides facing and raw edges aligned, stitch together large squares, using ¼-inch seam allowance, to make basket quartet. Press seams open.

9. Using small handstitch shown below, appliqué basket handles in place; remove basting. Press top flat (it should measure 11 inches square).

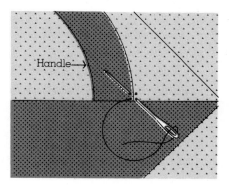

Handle →

Making the pillow

1. Cut 1-inch decorative border into four pieces, two 11 inches long and two 12 inches long. With right sides facing, pin and stitch short border pieces to opposite edges of patchwork top piece, using ¼-inch seam allowance. Press seams toward border. Attach long border pieces to remaining edges of top piece in same way.

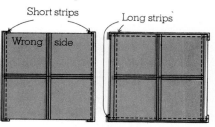

Short strips   Long strips

Wrong side

2. From solid fabric, measure, mark, and cut four border strips, two 12 by 2½ inches and two 16 by 2½ inches; for zipper in edge, make one long border strip 2¾ inches deep. Following same procedure as in step 1, stitch these borders to narrow decorative borders, beginning with shorter borders on edges with shorter narrow borders. Press seams toward border.

3. From solid fabric, measure, mark, and cut a 16-inch square for pillow bottom if pillow opening will be handstitched closed. For zipper in edge, cut a bottom piece 16 by 16¼ inches; for zipper centered in pillow bottom, cut a bottom piece 16 by 17½ inches.

4. See "Knife-edge pillow with welt," steps 2–4, pages 17–18, to baste welt to top piece.
   To install zipper in edge, see "Lapped zipper in welted edge," pages 13–14. For zipper centered in pillow bottom, see "Lapped zipper in pillow bottom or unwelted edge," pages 12–13.
   See "Knife-edge pillow with welt," steps 6 and 7, page 18, to stitch pieces together and finish pillow. *Note: When basting welt and stitching pieces together, use ½-inch seam allowances.*

Breakfast-in-bed bolsters

What could be more blissful than to linger in bed propped up against this fresh floral backrest? The beauty of these four bolsters is that they tie together in a comfy armchair arrangement for breakfast or reading in bed. Then, after you're up and about, you can untie them and use them like regular bolsters.

Gather together...

For four bolsters:

1 full-size flat sheet with decorative border

3 packages "wide" bias tape (1½ inches wide when unfolded) in accent color

4 cylindrical foam bolster forms, one 9 by 32 inches, one 8 by 32 inches, and two 8 by 15 inches (see "Forms & fillers," pages 8–9)

2½ yards 50-inch-wide, or 3½ yards 31-inch-wide bonded polyester batting (See "Forms & fillers," pages 8–9)

Two 29-inch zippers and two 12-inch zippers in color to match sheet (optional)

Wrapping the forms

1. See "Polyurethane foam," page 9, to wrap foam forms with polyester batting.

Making the bolsters

1. Cut off decorative border on sheet, then cut border in half crosswise for two ties.

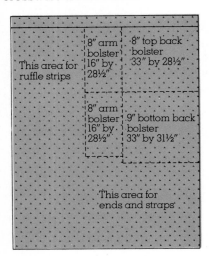

This area for ruffle strips

8" arm bolster 16" by 28½"

8" top back bolster 33" by 28½"

8" arm bolster 16" by 28½"

9" bottom back bolster 33" by 31½"

This area for ends and straps

Measure, mark, and cut pieces from remaining sheet, as shown. If you plan to install zippers, add ½ inch to short dimension of each bolster piece.

One 33 by 28½-inch piece (top back)

One 33 by 31½-inch piece (bottom back)

Two 16 by 28½-inch pieces (arms)

Six 9-inch circles (ends)

Two 10-inch circles (ends)

Six 2½ by 86-inch strips (ruffles—piece strips for necessary length)

Two 2½ by 95-inch strips (ruffles—piece strips for necessary length)

Eight 3-inch-wide pieces; length should equal border width, plus 1 inch (straps)

2. Unfold bias tape and press flat; refold in half lengthwise and press new crease. Place one bolster piece right side up. With raw edges aligned and fold toward bolster's center, lay folded strip of bias tape along each short edge on top and back pieces and along each long edge on arm pieces. Machine baste tape within seam allowance; topstitch tape close to fold. Repeat on other pieces.

3. If bolster openings will be handstitched closed, pin long edges, with right sides facing and raw edges aligned. Stitch a short seam at each end, leaving most of edge open to insert form. Backstitch at beginning and end of seams. Along opening, press back seam allowances to make sharp, straight creases for later handstitching. See "Lapped zipper in pillow bottom or unwelted edge," pages 12–13, to install zippers in lengthwise seams, if desired. Keep in mind that bolster piece is tube-shaped and that there is no top or bottom piece.

4. With right sides facing, pin and stitch together short ends of one ruffle strip to form loop. Fold in half lengthwise, right side out, and press to make double-thickness loop. Working along raw edges, pin 1-inch-wide box pleats; pin pleated loop to right side of bolster edge, adjusting as necessary to make loop fit. Machine baste to bolster edge, using ½-inch seam allowance. Repeat with other loops.

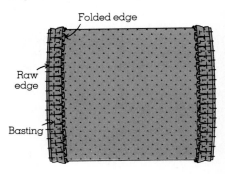

Folded edge

Raw edge

Basting

5. For each strap (four in all), pin together two strap pieces, with right sides facing. Using ½-inch seam allowance, stitch around edges, leaving an opening for turning. Turn right side out, press, and handstitch (see page 14) opening closed.

6. On right side of one 9-inch end piece, position two straps as shown. Topstitch across ends of straps. Repeat on another 9-inch end piece.

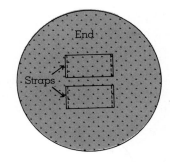

End

Straps

7. From scraps of sheet (piecing as necessary), measure and mark two strips to line border ties; cut strips. With right sides facing, pin border ties to lining strips. Stitch, using ½-inch seam allowance and mitering ends for pointed ties; leave openings for turning. Turn ties right side out, press, and handstitch openings closed.

8. Keep 10-inch end pieces and largest bolster piece (bottom back) together; remaining end pieces will fit remaining bolster pieces. Fold raw edges at ends of one bolster piece and matching end pieces in quarters and mark divisions on edges. With right sides facing and end piece up, match marks on bolster piece to marks on end piece and pin pieces together. (Make sure you pin each end piece with straps to each short bolster piece.) With end piece up, stitch around circumference, using ½-inch seam allowance and making sure pleats are smooth and flat as you stitch. Repeat with other bolster and end pieces.

9. Turn each bolster right side out and insert form. Zip closed; or, for stitched closure, pin open edges together and handstitch closed.

10. Slip ties through straps on each arm bolster. To assemble backrest, place arm bolsters at right angles to 9-inch back bolster, as shown in photo. Wrap ties once around back bolster and cross; place 8-inch back bolster on top, and wrap and knot ties around it.

Lean back in luxury against bolsters fit for a reclining queen. Covered in floral bedsheet fabric, they're linked in an armchair arrangement by wide ties sewn from the sheet's decorative border. Design: Phyllis Dunstan.

Index

Boldface numbers refer to color
photographs

Appliqué, **44**, 56, **56**, **57**,
   57–58, 60–61, 62, **63**, **64**,
   64–65, **65**
Art nouveau pillow, 62, **63**

Blindstitch, 14
Blocking needlepoint, 15–16
Bolsters, 30–31, **38**, **47**, **48**, **49**,
   78–79, **79**
Borders, 24–26, 35, **38**, **39**, **41**,
   42, **44**, **45**–47, 60–61, 62,
   63, **74**, 75, 76–77
Boxed cushion, 28–29, **33**, **36**,
   37, **39**, **48**, **49**, 68–69, **71**
Boxing strips, 8, 28–29
Breakfast-in-bed bolsters,
   78–79, **79**
Butterfly-corner pillow, 19–20,
   35

Chalk, 5
Child-designed pillows, 56, **56**
Crewel embroidery, **58**, 59
Crewel landscape pillows, **58**,
   59
Cushions, 28–29, **33**, **36**, **37**,
   39, **48**, **49**, 68–69, **71**
Cutting, measuring &
   marking, 7–8

Down, 9

Early American stencil pillow,
   74, 75
Embroidery, 51–53, **55**, **58**, 59
Embroidery scissors, 5
Enlarging & transferring
   patterns, 15

Fabric, 5–8
Fabric calculations & cutting,
   7–8
Fibers, fabric & care, 5–6
Fillers & forms, 8–9
Filling, polyester, 9
Flanges, 23–24, **34**, **38**, **47**
Floor pillows, **40**, **41**
Foam, polyurethane, 9
Forms & fillers, 8–9

Gathered welt, 11
Gift-wrapped pillows, **50**,
   50–51

Handstitches, 14
Herbal heirloom pillows,
   51–53, **55**

Ironing tools, 5

Kapok, 9
Knife-edge pillow, 16–18, **33**,
   38, **40**–42, **43**, **44**, **45**, **47**,
   50, **50**, 51–53, 54, **55**, 56,
   56, **58**, 59, 60–61, 62, **63**,
   66, 66–67, **72**, 72–73, **73**,
   74, 75, 76–77

Lemon & orange chair pillow,
   73, **73**
Let a child design your pillow,
   56, **56**

Mat, tube-quilted, 70, **71**
Measuring, marking & cutting,
   7–8
Measuring tools, 4–5
Mitered-corner borders, 24–26,
   35, **38**, **39**, **46**, **47**, **74**, 75
Mock-box pillow, 18, **33**, **34**, **35**,
   39, **46**, **57**, 57–58, **64**,
   64–65, **65**
Mola pillow, 60–61, **63**

Natural fibers, 6
Needlepoint, 15–16
Needles, 5

Painted pillows, **42**, **43**, **72**,
   72–73
Patchwork, **45**, **74**, 76–77
Patterns, 15
Pillow projects, 50–79
   Art nouveau pillow, 62, **63**
   Breakfast-in-bed bolsters,
      78–79, **79**
   Crewel landscape pillows,
      58, 59
   Early American stencil
      pillow, **74**, 75
   Gift-wrapped pillows, **50**,
      50–51
   Herbal heirloom pillows,
      51–53, **55**
   Lemon & orange chair
      pillow, 73, **73**
   Let a child design your
      pillow, 56, **56**
   Mola pillow, 60–61, **63**
   Printed & painted pillows,
      72, 72–73
   Quartet of patchwork
      baskets, **74**, 76–77
   Ribbon-linked pillow train,
      57, 57–58
   Shiki-buton, 68–69, **71**
   Smocked pillow, **66**, 66–67
   Summer & winter pillows,
      64, 64–65, **65**
   Tube-quilted mat, 70, **71**
   Woven ribbon pillow, 54, **55**
Pillows, style variations, 16–27
   borders, 24–26, **35**, **38**, **39**,
      41, **42**, **44**, **45**–47, 60–61,
      62, **63**, **74**, 75, 76–77
   butterfly-corner, 19–20, **35**
   flanges, 23–24, **34**, **38**, **47**
   knife-edge, 16–18, **33**, **38**,
      40–42, **43**, **44**, **45**, **47**, 50,
      50, 51–53, 54, **55**, 56, **56**,
      58, 59, 60–61, 62, **63**, **66**,
      66–67, **72**, 72–73, **73**, **74**,
      75, 76–77
   mock-box, 18, **33**, **34**, **35**, **39**,
      46, **57**, 57–58, **64**, 64–65, **65**
   puff, 21–22

Pillows, style variations (cont'd.)
   ruffles, 26–27, 54, **55**, **66**,
      66–67, 78–79, **79**
   shams, 22–23, **46**, **47**, **48**
   soft-box, 19
   sunburst, 21, **35**, **39**
   Turkish-corner, 20–21, **33**, **34**,
      36, **37**, **43**
Pillow shams, 22–23, **46**, **47**, **48**
Pins, 5
Polyester filling, 9
Polyurethane foam, 9
Preshrinking, 6
Pressing, 6
Printed & painted pillows, **42**,
   43, **72**, 72–73
Printed pillows, **42**, **72**, 72–73
Puff pillow, 21–22

Quartet of patchwork baskets,
   74, 76–77
Quilting, 70

Rectangular bolster, 30
Rectangular pieces, cutting, 7
Ribbon-linked pillow train, **57**,
   57–58
Round bolster, 30–31, **38**, **47**,
   48, **49**, 78–79, **79**
Round pieces, cutting, 8
Ruffles, 26–27, 54, **55**, **66**,
   66–67, 78–79, **79**
Ruler, 5

Sewing machine, 5
Sewing tools & supplies, 4–5

Shams, 22–23, **46**, **47**, **48**
Shears, 5
Shiki-buton, 68–69, **71**
Shirred boxing, 28–29, **36**, **47**
Shopping for fabric, 6
Smocked pillow, **66**, 66–67
Soft-box pillow, 19
Square-corner border, 26, **41**,
   42, **44**, **45**, 60–61, 62, **63**,
   74, 76–77
Square pieces, cutting, 7
Stenciling, **74**, 75
Summer & winter pillows, **64**,
   64–65, **65**
Sunburst pillow, 21, **35**, **39**
Synthetic fibers, 6

Thread, 6
Ties, 14–15, **33**, **73**
Transferring & enlarging
   patterns, 15
Tube-quilted mat, 70, **71**
Tufting, 15, **35**, **39**
Turkish-corner pillow, 20–21,
   33, **34**, **36**, **37**, **43**

Wedge bolster, 30, **49**
Welt, 9–11
Whipstitch, 14
Woven ribbon pillow, 54, **55**

Yardstick, 4

Zipper foot, 5
Zippers, 11–14

Decorative details in cutwork embroidery make an eyelet-ruffled sham special; solid-color knife-edge pillow peeks through, accenting floral motifs. Design: Naomie Cardoza.